WHY MARY?

FROM A MOTHER'S HEART, A FRESH PERSPECTIVE

Sharon F. Lawlor

WESTBOW
PRESS®
A DIVISION OF THOMAS NELSON
& ZONDERVAN

Copyright © 2016, 2017 Sharon F. Lawlor.
Visit Sharon Lawlor at www.sharonlawlor.com.
Email: info@sharonlawlor.com.

Edited by Dr. Dennis E. Hensley

All rights reserved. No part of this book may be used or reproduced by any means, graphic, electronic, or mechanical, including photocopying, recording, taping or by any information storage retrieval system without the written permission of the author except in the case of brief quotations embodied in critical articles and reviews.

WestBow Press books may be ordered through booksellers or by contacting:

WestBow Press
A Division of Thomas Nelson & Zondervan
1663 Liberty Drive
Bloomington, IN 47403
www.westbowpress.com
1 (866) 928-1240

Because of the dynamic nature of the Internet, any web addresses or links contained in this book may have changed since publication and may no longer be valid. The views expressed in this work are solely those of the author and do not necessarily reflect the views of the publisher, and the publisher hereby disclaims any responsibility for them.

Cover Photo: Accent Portraits by Diana, San Juan Capistrano, CA,
info@accentportraitsbydiana.com

Scripture quotations taken from the New American Standard Bible® (NASB), Copyright © 1960, 1962, 1963, 1968, 1971, 1972, 1973, 1975, 1977, 1995 by The Lockman Foundation Used by permission. www.Lockman.org

ISBN: 978-1-5127-8846-4 (sc)
ISBN: 978-1-5127-8848-8 (hc)
ISBN: 978-1-5127-8847-1 (e)

Library of Congress Control Number: 2017907623

Print information available on the last page.

WestBow Press rev. date: 8/3/2017

Listen to the lambs
All a cryin'
I want to go to heaven
When I die.

Traditional Spiritual

This book is dedicated to the memory of Dr. Robert Saucy, who looked past my gender and age to see the call of God on my life. His encouragement to "speak with authority" gave me the courage to write this book. His caution not to be the only voice led me to research the early days of the church, where I found the confirmation he required. My gratitude is insufficient for all he taught me during my time at the Talbot School of Theology. I rejoice in the knowledge he will receive his reward in heaven for every life changed through this work.

Contents

Preface xi
Acknowledgments xiii
Introduction xv

PART I: THE EMPRESS WHO LOVED THE VIRGIN

Chapter 1 1
Chapter 2 9
Chapter 3 11
Chapter 4 17
Chapter 5 21
Chapter 6 27
Chapter 7 31
Chapter 8 39

PART II: THE DEVELOPMENT OF MARIAN DEVOTION: PULCHERIA TO VATICAN II

Chapter 9 51
Chapter 10 61
Chapter 11 65
Chapter 12 75
Chapter 13 81
Chapter 14 87
Chapter 15 93
Chapter 16 101

Chapter 17.. 105
Chapter 18...119

Part III: A Biblical Response to Marian Tradition and Practice

Chapter 19.. 127
Chapter 20 135
Chapter 21.. 157

Part IV: Why Jesus

Chapter 22...175

Epilogue.. 187
References.. 189
Bibliography 199
Appendix.. 207

Preface

One of the first classes I had in seminary (M.A. Bible Exposition, 2007) was Methods of Research. We were required to write three thesis statements on topics that interested us. The first two were easy, but I was at a loss for the third. At that point I was not really sure why God had even called me to seminary! *I'm a woman! I'm too old to learn new things, especially Hebrew and Greek!* Now I had to come up with yet a third theological topic? I was stumped.

It had become my regimen to read through the Bible each year. The morning before the assignment was due I read Simeon's prophecy concerning Jesus, which was given when Mary and Joseph presented the infant Jesus in the temple.

> And Simeon blessed them, and said unto Mary, his mother, Behold, this child is set for the fall and rising again of many in Israel; and for a sign which shall be spoken against. (Yea, a sword shall pierce through thy own soul also,) that the thoughts of many hearts may be revealed. (Luke 2:34–35 KJV)

I thought it strange that this personal comment to Mary would be in parenthesis. Here was my third thesis question! And that is the one the professor approved.

My initial research was cursory (this was only a one-credit class). Everything I found said that the sword was the pain that Mary would feel when she saw her Son suffer and die on the cross, so that was my initial conclusion. But that conclusion bothered me. As a mom, I knew that any time one of my children was physically injured, no matter how minor the injury, I felt a physical pain myself. Surely this prophecy—in the middle of such a profound statement about the Savior of the world—must mean something more. Throughout the remainder of my study on Bible exposition, the verse remained a mystery. I graduated without answering that question.

An advisor suggested I pursue a Ph.D., but that was not a financial or logical possibility. I could, however, pursue a Th.M. (Master of Theology) degree at the seminary I had been attending. Again, a research class was required, and I needed a topic. The day it was due I was driving to class and received a call from a man who had been part of a spiritual warfare class I had taught that summer. He was experiencing an attack of demonic oppression that made it unable for him to eat or sleep. As soon as I parked the car, we prayed together over the phone. His faith gave him victory over the evil presence. When he was finally able to speak, he said the spirit was somehow connected to his visit to the shrine of the Virgin Mary at Lourdes: Mary, again! When I went into class I knew my thesis would be on the sword that pierced the heart of Mary.

I arranged to take a one-on-one, in-depth class on Catholic theology with my Th.M. mentor, Dr. Robert Saucy, and I began my research in earnest. Where did the veneration of Mary start? How did Mary become such a significant part of the Catholic Economy of Salvation when so little was said about her in Scripture and the early church? Three years of research led me to an answer. An additional year of research was required to write this book. I pray that you are blessed by it, as I have been in its writing.

If you are touched by this book, please let me know. I may be reached through my website at www.sharonlawlor.com.

Acknowledgments

Part I, the dramatization of the story of Empress Pulcheria, a Catholic saint, could not have been written without the foundation provided in *Theodosian Empresses* by Kenneth G. Holum. If you are fond of history, I strongly recommend his book, as his research is excellent.

Part II, a further tracing of the history of the development of Marian veneration in the Catholic Church, had a similar foundation in *Mary* by Hilda Graef. Ms. Graef was extremely gifted in languages and a perfectionist in detail. Her reporting on this history was not influenced by her Catholic faith: she was straightforward in recording when ancient scholars disagree. The most recent edition includes a section on Vatican II written by Thomas A. Thompson, SM, and should be on the shelf of any serious Marian scholar.

My sincere thanks go to those who prayed for me through this project: you know who you are. God will credit to your account all those whose lives are touched by it. The same is true for those of you who donated to help cover the cost of publishing: may God reward you a hundredfold.

To my Accountability Group, Lynne Leite, Judy Stapp, and Nancy Williams: those monthly meetings continue to bear fruit! Thank you for all of your encouragement and practical advice.

Last, but not least, I want to recognize my husband for his patience and for all of the mornings he got his own coffee, the first and second cup!

Introduction

Throughout the world one can find evidence of the love people have for Mary, the mother of Jesus, the one many recognize as the Savior of the world. From magnificent cathedrals to small roadside shrines where the faithful followers of Mary leave flowers and prayers, the devotion to Mary is evident. Rosaries can be seen in the hands of her followers in nearly every continent, and the number of people who seek her intercession on their behalf continues to grow.

Where did this love for the mother of Jesus Christ begin? The Gospel of Luke, chapter 1, records Mary's visit to her cousin Elizabeth. Elizabeth addresses Mary as "blessed among women." Mary states, "All generations will count me blessed," because she was chosen by God to bear the long-awaited, prophesied Messiah, the Savior of the world. These two statements point to recognition of the singular blessing God gave to this one woman among all the women who ever lived: she would bear the Son of God, Jesus Christ, who would be born to a virgin, Mary, and would not have an earthly father—just as God had prophesied in Genesis 3:15. Yet, the recognition of God's blessing on Mary—that He chose her to bear His only begotten Son—goes beyond mere acknowledgment in the hearts and actions of those who adore her.

Mary is venerated as not only the mother of Jesus the Christ but also, by millions of Catholic faithful, as the Mother of the Church, the intercessor between mankind and her Son. How did this humble maiden, the "handmaid of the Lord," become the recipient of such great devotion and become the focal point of so many prayers?

We see the seeds of this devotion while Jesus was engaged in His earthly ministry. Luke records an event that occurred while Jesus was correcting the Pharisees' accusations regarding the source of His ability to cast out demons. A woman in the crowd cried out, "Blessed is the womb that bore you and the breasts at which you nursed." Jesus corrected her saying, "On the contrary, blessed are those who hear the word of God and observe it" (Luke 11:27–28).

Scripture records Mary's presence with the disciples as they followed Jesus from place to place, her presence at the foot of the cross when Jesus was crucified, and her presence in the upper room when God poured out His Holy Spirit on the followers of Christ. Aside from these instances, we do not see any biblical evidence that Mary held a special place in the reverence, faith, or practice of the early church.

We do see evidence for the devotion to Mary that was proposed by the woman in the crowd in other places in the world where goddess worship had been previously practiced. Ancient hymns to Mary echoing goddess worship can be found as far away as Ethiopia, Egypt, and Spain. One of the earliest churches erected in Mary's honor was built in Ephesus, where she lived with John, the disciple whom Jesus loved and into whose care Jesus had entrusted His mother. The book of Acts records Ephesus as the seat of devout goddess worship during the time of Paul. The growth of Christianity in Ephesus led to a reduction in the idol maker's profits and led to the riot recorded in Acts 19:23–41.

The very human desire to venerate the mother of our Lord, while not seen to any great extent in the earliest scriptures, in fact, occurred wherever the good news of Jesus was preached and goddess worship was common. The virtue of virginity as a hallmark of goddesses became a hallmark of Mary as well.

By the fifth century Mary had obtained a place of prominence in the spiritual life of many Christians, primarily those who worshipped in the Catholic tradition. This book begins with a story that describes how the devotion of one young girl became the seed of devotion to Mary. It goes on to provide an historical account of how the seeds of her devotion grew to a belief embraced by millions around the world.

How does that devotion compare to the biblical picture of faith that God expects from us? What is Mary's true place in the order of salvation? These questions and more will be answered in the final chapters. I pray that you will find blessing and renewed zeal for your faith.

Part I

The Empress Who Loved the Virgin

Chapter 1

The old priest stood in the alcove by the door to the children's wing of the palace and watched Pulcheria as she schooled her younger siblings. What a difference the past four years had made in the little girl!

He remembered the first time he saw her from this very spot. She had been sitting, alone, on the old iron bench, surrounded by the most beautiful garden. There five-year-old Pulcheria wept in agonizing sobs, mourning the loss of her dear mother, the beloved Empress Aelia Eudoxia.

Who was he to comfort such a sad, broken spirit? This poor little one needed a nurse, not an old priest! Yet, her father, Emperor Arcadius, had insisted the children needed to have a Christian education above all else. Even today, the memories of the poor, lonely, weeping child tugged at his heart.

Pulcheria did not like the old priest at all. When he was introduced to the children, she was quick to remind her father of her mother's dying words: Pulcheria was to oversee the care of her younger sisters and brother. Even haughty Antiochus, her brother's official tutor, let her oversee playtime in the nursery, didn't he? Overhearing this exchange, the old priest knew he would have to win the little one's heart if he were to keep his position in the palace. Her father, the emperor, clearly doted on his daughter.

The old priest quickly realized this was no ordinary little girl! Pulcheria was smart. She not only learned her lessons quickly, she never forgot anything she learned. And she was not just clever when it came to lessons. Pulcheria grasped social ideas as well. She seemed to understand, from a very young age, how to manipulate people's affections and actions. In fact, she reminded him a lot of himself at her age. He knew from his own experience that there was one way he could entice her to interact with him.

He would promise to teach her to read so that she could teach her sisters and brother.

One morning as he watched the forlorn child sitting alone in the garden, he contemplated how best to teach her. He recalled the lessons he had received at the feet of his own teacher, Bishop Athanasius. The bishop had said a worthy life for a girl would be organized around the life of Mary, the mother of Jesus Christ. At the time, the priest had thought this lesson had no relevance for him, but now he understood. This was the perfect teaching for a little one who grieved so for her mother! And this path would surely please the emperor!

As he expected, Pulcheria's interest was soon captured. She proved to be a very eager student, constantly seeking to know more about her favorite subject. Her devotion to the Virgin Mary became her obsession. As her academic skills increased, so did her desire to read everything she could obtain. The old priest was driven by her passion to seek everything he could find on the mother of Jesus Christ. Pulcheria's passion for these stories drove her desire to be able to read them in Latin and Greek, and she quickly mastered both languages.

Not surprisingly, the girl's second favorite subject proved to be her own mother. She diligently sought anyone who would tell her stories about Empress Eudoxia. This topic was not one the old priest encouraged. John Chrysostom, archbishop of Constantinople, had preached against women overstepping their bounds, a clear reference to Eudoxia's influence over the emperor. The empress and archbishop's hatred of each other was vehement and passionate. When Chrysostom criticized the lavish lifestyle of the royal court, Eudoxia called for him to be banished from the city

At age four Pulcheria was old enough to remember the fear that swept through the royal household as the people of the city rioted in objection to the ousting of their bishop. The fire they set in the Great Church had spread to the palace. Eudoxia took the children into the tunnels to hide. The dampness of the tunnels and the stress of seeing their usually strong mother acting in fear had terrified the children. Pulcheria's older sister was taken ill and died. Fearing this was God's punishment, Eudoxia called for the return of Archbishop Chrysostom. The ensuing peace was short-lived.

Pulcheria remembered the wonderful celebration that was made a few months later when her father placed a beautiful silver statue of her mother in the town square. How proud she had been of her mother that day! The statue glistened in the sun. It seemed to radiate the beauty of her mother. But the archbishop was not pleased.

Chrysostom vehemently denounced the ceremony the emperor had organized in his beloved wife's honor.[1] The archbishop's objection centered on the formation and placement of the statue; the city square was adjacent to the Church of the Apostles, referred to by the people as the Great Church. The ceremony of dedication, in Chrysostom's eyes, looked like devotion that should be given only to God, not to idols.

In response, Eudoxia called for her husband to convene a synod to evict Chrysostom, who had preached a sermon on the biblical account of Herodias asking for the head of John the Baptist.[2] It was clear to all who heard it that he was referring to the empress. Acceding to her request, Emperor Arcadius deposed the archbishop and banished him from the city. On Easter, government troops attacked and killed many who went to the Great Church to be baptized by the archbishop. Riots ensued and spread to other cities.[3] Because Pulcheria possessed keen awareness and an insatiable curiosity, the old priest knew she was aware of all of these things.

The night Chrysostom was to leave, there was a violent hailstorm. Pulcheria was with her mother when Eudoxia went into early labor and soon miscarried her sixth child. The events of the past month had exhausted her.[4] Just before she died, she entrusted the care of the younger children to her young daughter.

Pulcheria adored her mother for her strength in standing up to the men in her life. She blamed the archbishop for her mother's death. From that night on she carried in her pocket a coin showing her mother crowned by the hand of God. The priest remembered she had held that very coin in her hand the morning he found her weeping in the garden.

Now that she was nine, he thought she should let go of her childish emotions. Instead, they intensified. The old priest was horrified by the little girl's hatred toward the head of the Church. He tried, diligently, to use the example of the Virgin Mary's humility and obedience to sway the child's thinking about the respect due the archbishop's position. But Pulcheria could not be convinced. She believed Chrysostom to be responsible for her mother's death. The priest found himself walking a very thin line between his devotion to the Church and his love of his position as the children's overseer. Though he tried to guide Pulcheria toward a submissive attitude, she was too much like her earthly mother.

In spite of his misgivings, the old priest was amazed at the transformation the girl had undergone since the day his heart was captivated by the dear little child weeping in the garden. Pulcheria was an exceptional child.[5] Not only could she remember everything she had ever read, she could cite both the book and the location of the passages. She was also an adept and compassionate teacher, and she had insisted on taking over the teaching of her younger siblings.

The younger children adored their sister. She mothered them with tenderness, yet expected them to be as diligent as she was about their studies. Arcadia, sixteen months younger, was devoted to her older sister, embracing her passion for the study of the Virgin Mary. Eudoxia's youngest daughter, Mariana, had been the recipient of Pulcheria's most tender care since just before her first birthday, when their mother died. Mariana's strong resemblance to their beloved older sister, Flacilla, who had died when Pulcheria was only three, contributed to the warm feelings Pulcheria had for her.

Her younger brother, Theodosius, however, received Pulcheria's most diligent attention. He had been proclaimed co-emperor by his father when he was only ten months old. Emperor Arcadius had made this proclamation in an effort to secure the ties to the Persian king, whose representative to the court was a young man named Antiochus.[6] Antiochus was appointed the boy's official guardian and took charge of his education. However, Antiochus was a very ambitious man. He was far too busy ingratiating himself with Anthemius,[7] the prefect of the household, to spend much time teaching the boy. In public he was a model subject in the emperor's service. In private, he was critical of Emperor Arcadius and the way Anthemius could sway the emperor's opinions. Antiochus's extensive engagement in court politics left him little time for anything else.

Though Antiochus neglected his responsibility in the children's wing of the palace, Emperor Arcadius was a frequent visitor. He doted on his daughters and delighted in the antics of his son. However, when Eudoxia died after the stillbirth of their sixth child, it was too painful for him to see them. In the year following her death, he went to the nursery on only a handful of occasions.

The children would have remained solely under the care of the old priest, seeing their grieving father only occasionally, if it were not for Pulcheria's persistence. She was much like her mother in temperament. Her father could not resist his daughter's requests for stories about his beloved wife for very long. For three years, whenever he could make time, he regaled her with stories about Eudoxia's accomplishments in the court, the love the people had for her, and the power she wielded in the affairs of the Church. Pulcheria listened raptly to these stories and joyfully passed them along to her siblings.

While the stories about Eudoxia's involvement in Church matters distressed the old priest, he could not stop Pulcheria from retelling them, because the emperor would be displeased. The child wielded quite a strong influence on her father! Whenever the priest heard Pulcheria telling the young children the stories, he tried to distract her with a new history book or promise of fabric for a new dress—another of Pulcheria's passions. The castle library blossomed with volumes appropriate for a young girl, mostly stories of the Virgin and saints of the Church, as the priest tried to stay one step ahead of her. But the volumes of history and government soon outnumbered them.

When it became clear Pulcheria's influence over her brother was as great as Eudoxia's influence over her husband, the old priest realized a stronger hand than his was necessary to rein her in. Risking the wrath of the "empress of the nursery," he reached out to Antiochus. When Antiochus at first failed to respond, the priest sent him a note threatening to expose him and his opinions to the prefect, Anthemius, who was the emperor's confidant and second-in-command.

When Antiochus finally appeared in the nursery to take charge of Theodosius's education, Pulcheria was furious! Her tantrum lasted three days. She screamed. She threw things. She refused to eat. A week had gone by since she'd summoned her father. Arcadius became worried and went to see if she was all right.

The emperor found the nursery in a terrible state. The children were sullen, refusing to eat, because they followed Pulcheria's example. Pulcheria was curled up in a ball on her bed, hair uncombed and eyes red from weeping. The old priest had heard the emperor was coming and had quickly sent word to Antiochus, repeating the threat to expose him if Antiochus did not intervene with the emperor on his behalf.

Seeing her father, Pulcheria's spirits lifted immediately. She knew her father would be devastated to see her in such a state. After all, he had already lost two children and his beloved wife. Pulcheria knew how much he adored her, and she knew she could use this adoration in her favor.

Weaving a tale of how the loss of her close ties to her brother would lead to her death of a broken heart, Pulcheria succeeded in getting her father and Antiochus to allow her to accompany Theodosius to all of his lessons. She made particular effort to smile at Antiochus and to praise his efforts at tutoring to her father every chance she got.

Antiochus had been directly responsible for selecting the old priest to serve as tutor for the children. He was aware of the weakness the emperor had exhibited when it came to the influence of his wife. He also saw how much Pulcheria resembled her mother in this regard. To ensure the heir to the throne would not be equally submissive to his older sister, Antiochus arranged for two sons of high-ranking court officials to be the boy's companions.

The two boys, Paulinus and Placitus,[8] proved to be no match for Pulcheria. Years later the hatred that developed between Paulinus and Pulcheria would lead to international intrigue. Pulcheria was clearly jealous about the time Theodosius spent with the boys.

Antiochus realized that it was important for the children, particularly Pulcheria, to look upon him affectionately. Because she had excelled in so many academic areas, Pulcheria was allowed to have some oversight of the boys' lessons. Antiochus thought this would pacify her and gain her favor. Allowing her this role would also set him free to return to his place in palace politics.

Pulcheria was delighted to take charge of the future emperor's education. She made it a point to learn everything she could about how an emperor should rule so she could teach him. She was determined that he would be a strong, honorable, just ruler. The stories she heard about their own father's weakness helped her see what would be undesirable in a future emperor. The histories she read about ancient kings inspired her to guide Theodosius's studies to ensure her brother would be an emperor of renown.

Because many of Theodosius's practical lessons about the court, palace, and community took place outside the palace walls, Pulcheria was liberated from the confines of the nursery. While Antiochus's attention was focused on the boy, Pulcheria cleverly used her beauty and wit to charm everyone with whom she came in contact, from the cook in the kitchen to visiting Church dignitaries.

Pulcheria quickly realized that Church leaders had great influence in the palace. She also remembered the power her mother had wielded over those leaders. Whenever she had the opportunity, Pulcheria delighted them with her knowledge of everything she learned from the old priest's books and stories about the apostles and the Virgin Mary.

By the time she was nine, Pulcheria had won the hearts of all who knew her. The old priest was distraught. Everyone believed she was a picture of perfection, but he saw her as a sly, conniving manipulator of people. He was very cautious around her and pretended to adore her as everyone else did. Pulcheria saw right through his charade.

Of all the people with whom she came in contact, the old priest was the only one Pulcheria was unable to win over completely. As intelligent as she was, she did not yet have the maturity to understand fully his reticence and mistrust.

Pulcheria truly believed she was a good girl! When she read the stories that described the Virgin Mary as a special child, she saw herself as no different. She earnestly believed she held the same place in God's grace as did the mother of Christ. Of course, there could only be one Christ, and, therefore, only one mother of Christ! But the little girl believed in her heart God had chosen her for a special role as well. When people adored her, she simply expected no less. When she manipulated people, she did so without thinking. She believed she was appointed by God to care for her brother as the holy mother, Mary, had cared for Christ, and she took her role very seriously. She did not see herself as the priest saw her. She could not understand why he sometimes looked at her with fear in his eyes. It made her feel angry, and she knew anger was sinful. She was obedient to him but avoided him as much as possible.

Chapter 2

It was a beautiful spring day when Pulcheria's world came crashing down again. Her father, Emperor Arcadius, who had fallen ill in the last part of the winter, died on May 1, 408.

Anthemius[1] and Antiochus[2] arrived together to take Theodosius from the children's wing to the emperor's rooms. It was well known Arcadius had named his son co-regent of the empire before he was a year old; he was the youngest person ever to hold the title. Now with the death of his father, he had become Theodosius II, emperor of the eastern half of the Roman Empire. He was seven years old.

Anthemius had held a great deal of influence over the emperor before he died. Because Theodosius was too young to rule, Anthemius became regent and assumed the title of praetorian prefect of the East. He was a gifted statesman. During the next six years he successfully defended the empire against a Hunnic invasion, he engendered peace between the Eastern and Western Roman Empires, and he doubled the size of the city of Constantinople by building the Theodosian walls, completing them in 414. The demands of ruling the empire left him little time to spend with the heir. The responsibility for oversight of the young emperor was again placed in the seemingly capable hands of Antiochus.

Professional teachers were hired to teach the young emperor more advanced methods of rhetoric, which Theodosius embraced. But Pulcheria[3] made sure he learned to present himself with imperial deportment. She asked Antiochus to provide Theodosius with riding masters and instructors in swordsmanship. When he was not engaged in these lessons she taught him the more practical skills: how to walk, sit, and manage his imperial garb while so engaged; how to contain his laughter and appropriately show gentleness and anger. She also told him all she had observed about how to appear knowledgeable about affairs of state even when he did not fully comprehend the subject. She knew that this skill would particularly be important when Anthemius arrived at the palace with documents for Theodosius to sign.

From her keen observation of people, Pulcheria knew these things were important if Theodosius were to take charge of the empire when he came of age. But even more essential, she believed, was his religious training. She impressed upon her brother the importance of worship with the people, spiritual discipline, works of charity, and regular discussions with important figures in the Church. She modeled much of this to him by her own actions. Following the traditions her mother had embraced, Pulcheria led her brother and sisters in prayer and reciting scripture in the morning and evening. On Wednesdays and Fridays, she insisted they refrain from eating meat and delicacies. She would not tolerate idleness among her siblings and ordered their free time tp be spent in activities that would benefit the poor and houses of prayer.

Life was simple and beautiful for the royal family as long as Pulcheria was given a wide responsibility to direct the education of her siblings. But that was about to change.

Chapter 3

Antiochus[1] had allowed Pulcheria great latitude in overseeing the education of her siblings while Emperor Arcadius was alive. The fact was, he was quite busy trying to make a name for himself in the imperial court. Like Anthemius, he was a man of great ambition.

After the emperor died, Antiochus used his position wisely as head of the royal household and overseer of the children wisely. He recognized the benefit of ingratiating himself with Anthemius. Because Anthemius continued to serve as Praetorian prefect, he was in charge of the army. As regent over the young emperor Theodosius II, Anthemius essentially ruled the Eastern Roman Empire. To be associated closely with Anthemius would, in turn, give Antiochus high standing in the imperial court.

Anthemius was dedicated to ruling the empire with all the skill and resources at his command. His work was admired by the people, and his statesmanship was respected by other leaders. Because Theodosius was only seven years old when he became emperor, Anthemius did not seriously consult with him on matters of state beyond taking him documents to sign. That began to change after the great celebration held in honor of the boy's tenth birthday.

It was on the occasion of this celebration that Theodosius II was formally introduced to his people. He had been thoroughly schooled by Pulcheria about how to address the people. His presentation was so effective that some of the imperial court marveled: his skill was quite beyond his years.

The celebration awakened the young emperor to the reality of his position. Pulcheria's excellent teaching began to take root and blossom. From that point, when Anthemius took documents for the emperor's official signature, Theodosius asked questions.

Antiochus was with Theodosius on one of these occasions. He saw how frustrated Anthemius got as the boy questioned every document he was to sign. When Anthemius was finally able to get away, Antiochus followed him out.

Anthemius was furious! In anger, he turned to Antiochus and blamed him for allowing the boy to take up so much of his valuable time. There was a country to run. Why did the boy think he had to ask questions anyway? He was too young to be involved in running the government!

Antiochus worried that Anthemius's rage would cost him his own position. "It is the girl, Pulcheria," Antiochus interjected. "She is encouraging him to learn to act like the emperor he is, even though he certainly is much too young. He adores her and will have me removed if I try to intervene."

"Well, something must be done," replied Anthemius angrily. "Perhaps we can give her something else to occupy her time. How old is she now?"

Antiochus began to grasp what Anthemius was thinking. "She is twelve years old."

Anthemius had just recently arranged the marriage of his daughter to a high-ranking military official in a neighboring country. Perhaps he could arrange a marriage for Pulcheria that would solidify his own position once Theodosius came of age to rule on his own. Antiochus knew his own future could be assured if he cooperated with Anthemius. They agreed to work toward finding a politically suitable husband for the young emperor's sister.

Meanwhile, Pulcheria's years of making friends with many classes of people throughout the city began to bear fruit. Discussions between Anthemius and his family regarding the possibility of one of his grandsons marrying the emperor's sister were overheard by the servants. They, in turn, shared this information with the palace servants. The entire serving class was aware of the affection the palace staff had for the girl because of the frequent kindnesses she showed to them and their families. They did not want her to learn of Anthemius's plans when she was being fitted for a wedding garment!

When Pulcheria learned about the plot to marry her off and eliminate her influence over her brother, she met the news with resolve and wisdom.[2] She had already been concerned that one of her sisters might marry an outsider, which could lead to unwanted obligations and competition for her brother's attention. Now she realized the first marriage might be her own. As a married woman she would be forced to leave her brother's side. Even worse, her husband would replace her as Theodosius's advisor. She remembered how Theodosius had relished his friendship with Paulinus and Placitus and had left her out of their games when they were younger. She knew she had to do something to keep another man from coming between her and her brother.

Pulcheria remembered that when her theological questions had become too difficult for her first teacher, the old priest, he had taken her to see Bishop Atticus at the Great Church. She knew the bishop's heart had been captivated by her childish innocence, grace, beauty, and ability to grasp deep theological ideas. Relying on his affection she arranged to meet with him and seek his advice.

When Pulcheria met with Atticus,[3] she poured out her heart to him with great weeping. She told him she did not want to marry. Her heart belonged to God, not men. She truly believed that just as Mary had been chosen to rear the Son of God, she had been chosen to rear her brother and be his guardian. Her sincerity and desperation struck the bishop deeply. He questioned her at length.

"Are you certain that you want to dedicate your virginity to God? Are you willing to give up the joy of bearing your own children to serve your brother's interests? Have you prayed and asked God if this is His will for your life?"

With each question, Pulcheria's resolve deepened. She would dedicate her virginity to God. She would dedicate her life to serving her brother's interests. Wasn't that what her mother meant when she charged Pulcheria with the care of her siblings?

After several hours and much soul searching of his own, Atticus agreed to accept and formalize Pulcheria's vow of virginity. Arrangements were made for a public celebration. Bans were posted in the church. Anthemius and Antiochus were so focused on their own plans, they did not realize what Pulcheria had done. When Isadorus, son of Anthemius and the mayor of Constantinople, notified his father of the upcoming ceremony, Anthemius ordered Antiochus to intervene. Antiochus refused to recognize Pulcheria's upcoming vow as one of godly resolve. He believed her actions were intended to secure her place of authority over her brother. He met with Bishop Atticus to try to secure his help in stopping the ceremony, but the bans had already been posted in the Great Church. It was too late.

The day Pulcheria formalized her vow was a day of celebration among the people of Constantinople. She arranged for the altar in the Great Church to be decorated with gold and precious stones. On it she called for an inscription dedicating her virginity and her brother's rule to God. Her first act upon returning to the palace was to ask her brother to banish Antiochus for his insult in questioning her vow.

During the last months of 412, Pulcheria spent a great deal of time with her family and the palace staff to solidify her authority. Realizing that her sisters could still be used as pawns, she encouraged them to take their own vows of virginity.

Using the stories she had read about Mary, the mother of Jesus Christ as her model,[4] Pulcheria[5] soon developed a large following of young women who also took the vow. Often these were daughters of wealthy families who had resources Pulcheria could draw on for charitable works. In addition, their families were powerful. These connections gave Pulcheria even more influence over the civil government. By March of 413 Isadorus had been replaced as mayor of Constantinople.

Pulcheria's hatred for Anthemius became unendurable. He continued to advise government affairs and appeared to accept Pulcheria's influence over Theodosius, but she could not forget he had tried to marry her to his grandson. By the spring of 414, she could no longer tolerate his presence. She informed her brother about the way Anthemius had taken power and had planned to have her removed from the palace through marriage. The last mention of Anthemius in the historical records was on April 18, 414.

With Anthemius and Isadorus gone, the army and the city were in need of leadership. Pulcheria remembered that Aurelian[6] had been dedicated to her mother. She had Theodosius call him out of retirement to become the Praetorian prefect of the East and mayor of Constantinople.

Anthemius had served as regent for Theodosius, who was still too young to take the throne officially. While Pulcheria had affection for Aurelian, because he had helped her mother, she did not believe he was capable of running the government. In her mind no one was more qualified for that position than the person who held it: her brother. She knew he was not yet of age; he still had much to learn, and she had much to teach him.

In the early summer of 414, Theodosius proclaimed his sister, Pulcheria, as Augusta (queen). Aurelian, as acting regent, likely tried to dissuade the

Why Mary?

boy. However, Pulcheria had impressed upon her brother that he was the one with the true authority. Theodosius was emboldened by his sister and ordered Aurelian to make the announcement.

The city enthusiastically embraced the celebration! Pulcheria was already adored by the people, thanks to her frequent forays into the city to deliver gifts to the poor personally. The beauty and grace of the young woman combined with her air of authority endeared her to powerful families as well as their servants. Only a few in the palace met this proclamation with scorn.

The proclamation announcing Augusta was considered a civil pronouncement rather than a spiritual one. Thus, the imperial palace, rather than the Great Church, was prepared for the ceremony. Flowers decorated every available space. Chefs were called in to prepare the feast. People of all classes vied for the opportunity to be part of the preparations.

This bustle of activity was in contrast to the normal mood of the palace. Dedicated to her faith, Pulcheria usually required that the palace resemble a monastery. However, she recognized the desire of the people to honor the occasion, so she loosened the rules, even allowing feasting to occur on the fasting days of Wednesday and Friday in the week leading up to the ceremony.

Early on July 4, 414,[7] Pulcheria went to the Great Church to pray and ask for Bishop Atticus's blessing. When she emerged, the people of the city greeted her with cheers and flowers as she made her way from the Great Church to the imperial palace. There her brother, Emperor Theodosius II, greeted her as Augusta and gave her the tokens of his authority to rule as regent in his place until he came of age.

Affirmations of her authority came quickly. In honor of her coronation, coins were struck with her image showing her being crowned by the hand of God. A Christmas sermon by Bishop Atticus titled "On Faith and Virginity" was dedicated to Pulcheria and her sisters. The third formal affirmation came on December 30, 414, when Aurelian placed a bust of Pulcheria in the senate house alongside those of her brother, emperor of the Eastern Roman Empire, and her father's brother, Honorius, emperor of the Western Roman Empire. This signified formal recognition of Pulcheria's equality with these emperors. She was sixteen.

Chapter 4

Pulcheria took her role as her brother's advisor very seriously.[1] To her, this was her spiritual calling. She truly believed that God had placed her above her brother to be his protector, teacher, and confidant. She felt connected to Mary, the mother of Jesus, in this way: just as Mary had been chosen to guide and direct the early life of the Son of God, so had Pulcheria been charged, by her mother, to guard, guide, and encourage her brother.

Theodosius adored his older sister and would have been content to let her lead while he pursued his reading and writing. But power and acclaim in her own name was not Pulcheria's goal. Unlike Anthemius, she never openly exhibited power or authority. From the very beginning of her reign she lifted her brother as the true emperor. She was so knowledgeable about the workings of civil government and so adept at reading the motives of people that when Theodosius II officially assumed the throne at age sixteen, she continued to advise him.

While all authority and power were attributed to Theodosius, the real power was in the hands of Pulcheria. Her vow of virginity, which she dedicated to the Virgin Mary, gave her a presence greater than that of the empresses before her. In the eyes of the people, she was more than their civil ruler; she was their spiritual example. In her youth, her followers had been her sisters. Now many women, especially those of wealth and power, followed her into a life of virginity consecrated to the memory of the Virgin Mary.

Pulcheria led these women by example. Her vow of chastity was matched by her vow to help the poor and suffering. The wealth and position of her followers made it possible for her to expand her charity beyond the walls of Constantinople.

Archbishop Atticus became both her advisor and encourager.² His own education in a monastery had led him finally to accept her vow of virginity. Her first teacher, the old priest, had distrusted Pulcheria's intelligence and aggressive personality. Atticus saw these things in a different light. He saw Pulcheria's dedication to Theodosius and the Virgin Mary.

O, if only all the people of Constantinople could have her dedication to the crown and the cross! he thought. Atticus contemplated how he might encourage the people to follow the pious example of this holy young woman.

With this intention in mind, Atticus did three things. First, at Pulcheria's request to honor Mary, he allowed her own royal robe to cover the altar she had dedicated when she was made Augusta. Once this was done, her robe became a regular part of the people's worship.

Second, again at Pulcheria's suggestion, a picture of Mary was painted above the altar in the Great Church. Because no one knew exactly what Mary looked like, and because Pulcheria embodied so much of what stories said of her, Pulcheria's own likeness was used as a model. The people were still in the habit of venerating statues and likenesses of royalty. With her likeness representing the Virgin Mary, the lines between civil government and religion dissolved.

By far the most powerful statement Atticus made was to allow the young empress to enter the altar area, a place reserved for holy men of God, and to take communion with the priests.

Atticus's efforts made it clear that in his mind anyone who opposed Pulcheria opposed the Virgin Mary. Because the term *Theotokos* (meaning Mother of God) had become a common title for Mary, the implication was that to oppose her was to oppose God Himself.

Though Pulcheria was careful to direct all attention regarding civil matters to her brother, she did not resist the veneration of the people in spiritual ones. Her spiritual influence was most evident in the imperial palace. She insisted that her brother and sisters serve as examples for the entire staff by rising early for prayer and singing hymns at her direction. Other regular times of daily prayer were also initiated by her. Fasting on Wednesdays and Fridays was strictly observed. The palace resembled a monastery.

Pulcheria's knowledge of history and her devotion to Mary ensured that spiritual matters would become a hallmark of the reign of Theodosius

II. Though Constantine had proclaimed Christianity to be the accepted religion, veneration of emperors was still common practice. Constantine's actions as civic head of the Church blurred the division between church and state. Pulcheria's influence moved the focus of power from the palace to the church.

Following the practice started by Constantine's mother, Helene, Pulcheria actively pursued relics of the saints and built chapels to house them. She spearheaded the building of churches dedicated to Mary. Whereas she did these things in the name of Theodosius, it was clear to all that it was she who possessed the fervent faith that drove these acquisitions.

While Pulcheria was the heart of the Eastern Roman Empire, Theodosius was the hand. Constantine had caused temple worship to cease by ending monetary donations. Pulcheria wanted all evidence of pagan worship removed. Acting out Pulcheria's zeal, Theodosius ordered the purging of even the foundations of the old temples.

The year after Theodosius elevated his sister to Augusta, he issued a constitution. This document reflected Pulcheria's fervor for Christianity. It ordered the removal of any pagan from public office and ordered all pagan priests to leave major cities and return to their villages; their property was confiscated and became property of the royal family. This document also forbade the building of new synagogues and ordered synagogues to be destroyed in places where their destruction would not cause rioting.[3]

The wording of this constitution emboldened Cyril, the new bishop of Alexandria, to lead a Christian mob against the city's Jewish population, destroying its synagogue and driving them from the city. When the Jews sent emissaries to Constantinople, however, they received no help. Cyril also sent emissaries, who said the Jewish people had instigated the conflict. Pulcheria stood with her brother in support of Cyril. Clearly the cause of Christianity was the highest priority for the royal family, and Pulcheria was the force that drove it.

So great was the love of the people for their empress that panegyrics, or hymns, celebrating her faith and virginity were written in her honor.[4] These hymns proclaimed her to be the mother of all who came to the Church through baptism as a result of her example. Rather than discouraging the singing of these hymns, Pulcheria embraced it. She saw it as God's approval of her spiritual leadership, which was endorsed by both Bishop Proclus and

Archbishop Atticus in sermons preached in the Great Church. She fully embraced the teaching of Atticus, who described Pulcheria and her virgins as "you who have been renewed in Christ, who have cast off every stain of sin and have partaken of blessing in the most holy Mary: you also may receive Him in the womb of faith."[5]

Proclus, who succeeded Atticus as bishop of Constantinople, praised her knowledge of salvation in Christ and her choice to serve the cross by and through her virginity. He said, "We wonder at the great soul of the empress, a brimming source of spiritual blessings for all. As long ago the Jews flung stones at Stephen, wishing to cast down the matchless preacher … so she devoted her virginity to Christ, exhausting her wealth in pious works."

The empress was touched and encouraged by his sermon. But the reference to the stoning of Stephen was disturbing. It pointed to the one blemish in the popularity of the empress: not everyone in Constantinople loved her. Pulcheria knew who her enemies were.

Chapter 5

The Christmas season had long been a favorite of Pulcheria's, for in this season, especially, Mary was a central figure. Daily prayers and hymns were still practiced in the rooms of the royal family; however, elsewhere, the somber atmosphere of the palace was lifted for a brief time. It was a time of hosting dignitaries and influential local families. Pulcheria's rule that no men were permitted in the Hebdomon Palace remained in place, but she agreed to attend the dinners with her brother.

Though she made every effort to be at her brother's side whenever he met with ambassadors from surrounding states, that had become increasingly difficult during the past couple of years. Theodosius was no longer a boy. While she knew he still yielded to her influence in most things, he had recently reconnected with his boyhood friend Paulinus, whom Pulcheria saw as a rival.

She knew that many men saw her influence over Theodosius as a roadblock to their own desire for power. By taking a vow of virginity, she had thwarted their attempt to disrupt her sway over her brother by arranging her marriage. At the same time, her charity toward the people engendered their love for the empress. The respect she enjoyed from the wives of the most influential men in the city made her position nearly indestructible. But Pulcheria also knew that her brother was a man. As emperor he would be expected to produce an heir. As he turned twenty, he began to listen to Paulinus' advice. With the Christmas festivities came many opportunities for Pulcheria's enemies to meet with Theodosius alone. Though she foresaw a coming rift with her brother, there was no way she could stop it.

The traditionalists, men who railed against Pulcheria's power, had long sought a way to remove her. Paulinus enlisted their help in finding a wife for

Theodosius who would represent their interests. Pulcheria also searched for a spouse for her brother. Unfortunately for her, most of the young women of marriageable age in Constantinople who were loyal to her had taken the vow of virginity. Pulcheria sent emissaries throughout the empire to seek a beautiful, well-educated woman to join the royal family. Paulinus and the traditionalists did the same. Then Paulinus learned that the perfect woman was right there in Constantinople.[1]

Athenais[2] was the daughter of a Greek pagan named Leontius, who moved his family to Constantinople, where he had built a successful business. He wanted his sons, Valerius and Gesius, to take over his business, and he established that in his will. His daughter was beautiful and intelligent; he expected to arrange a marriage for her that would solidify his standing among the powerful families of the city. Paulinus was diligently searching for a bride for Theodosius when Leontius died. His sons, unwilling to share their inheritance with Athenais, contacted Paulinus and invited him to meet their sister.

The most influential women of the city had learned about Leontius's daughter from their husbands and hurried to tell Pulcheria. The empress summoned Athenais to the palace and was impressed by the girl's beauty and intelligence, but also her humble demeanor. Athenais had heard of Pulcheria and was in awe. Her adoration was visible and touched Pulcheria's heart.

Pulcheria questioned Athenais about her faith and was appalled to learn the girl had been reared in a pagan family. However, because of the way her father and brothers treated her, Athenais had no loyalty to their religion. She wanted to please this beautiful, powerful woman and listened eagerly as Pulcheria spoke about Mary and Mary's son, the Savior, Jesus Christ. Convinced the girl could be converted to Christianity, Pulcheria arranged for Theodosius to meet Athenais.

When Paulinus heard Pulcheria had arranged a meeting between Theodosius and Athenais, he was overjoyed. He assured Valerius and Gesius that their sister would not retaliate once she became wife of the emperor. As Theodosius's friend, he would intervene on their behalf. He met with Theodosius and asked to be present to advise him when he met the girl, suggesting that a man's opinion in such a matter was infinitely more important than his sister's. Theodosius agreed, and the meeting was scheduled.

As Pulcheria and Paulinus expected, Theodosius fell in love with Athenais. He oversaw her conversion to Christianity and at her baptism renamed her Eudocia. Theodosius gave her brothers positions of authority in nearby cities and began a series of promotions for Paulinus that would eventually give him power in Constantinople that Pulcheria would never have allowed.

The wedding of Theodosius II and Eudocia was held in the Great Church on June 7, 421. The city rejoiced. Pulcheria and her sisters welcomed their new sister-in-law with a private dinner in the Hebdomon Palace. Theodosius was ecstatic. His sisters' acceptance of his new wife meant a great deal to him. His new bride stole his heart. No man could have been happier than Theodosius was that summer.

The emperor appreciated that Pulcheria cared enough for his new wife's position that she chose to move her living quarters to the Hebdomon Palace. He assured Pulcheria that his marriage would not change their relationship. To solidify that vow, he elicited her advice regarding the Roman-Sassanid war. When the war was over, he placed a victory column at the Hebdomon Palace, attributing the victory to his sisters' vow of virginity. Theodosius also fulfilled Pulcheria's wishes to have a golden cross studded with precious stones placed on Golgotha near Jerusalem. It appeared that he aimed to keep his vow to maintain his close relationship with his sister. However, Paulinus and the traditionalists had other plans.

Pulcheria's hope that her brother's wife would respond to her with the same adoration she'd exhibited at their first meeting was quickly dashed. What Eudocia admired was Pulcheria's power. An intelligent woman in her own right, and encouraged by Paulinus and others, Eudocia set out to replace her sister-in-law.

The first step was simple, and she didn't have to do a thing to accomplish it. In honor of their marriage, Theodosius had coins minted that showed Eudocia being crowned by the hand of God, similar to Pulcheria. Whereas this was upsetting to Pulcheria, she knew she could not intervene. This was a traditional custom, and she had personally schooled her brother in the importance of following imperial tradition.

Eudocia was wise enough to know that being Theodosius's wife did not give her sufficient leverage to cause a split between her husband and his sister. Fortunately her father, Leontius, had been a professor and had personally overseen her schooling in literature, philosophy, and rhetoric. As a result she was skilled in writing. Theodosius was widely known for similar skills; he was called the Calligrapher. The young woman made use of on this interest. Her praise of his knowledge and talent endeared her to him on an intellectual level with passion equal to that of the marriage chamber.

While her first child, Licinia Eudoxia, was not the heir she hoped to give her husband, the baby proved Eudocia was capable of doing so. In response to her promise to give him an heir, Theodosius proclaimed her Augusta. Thus, on January 2, 423, Eudocia replaced Pulcheria, at least officially. She knew that in reality Pulcheria still held a great deal of power behind the scenes.

Eudocia, coached by Paulinus at the behest of the traditionalists, had her uncle, Asclepiodotus, proclaimed Praetorian prefect of the East. Through his position and under the guidance of Eudocia, concessions were made, and pagans and Jews were given some leniency. Theodosius issued a constitution stating that Christians were not to injure nor persecute pagans or Jews as long as they lived quietly. In addition, any Christian who destroyed the property of one of these protected groups would have to make triple or quadruple restitution.

Pulcheria was furious. It was clear that Eudocia still had some loyalty to her pagan roots. The archbishop had been ailing, so Pulcheria sent word to Simeon, a monk famous for living on a pillar outside of Antioch. Simeon responded with a letter to Theodosius:

> Since you have grown arrogant and forgotten the Lord your God who gave you your diadem and the throne of the empire, and since you have become friend, comrade and protector of the faithless ... know now that you will soon face the punishment of divine justice, you and all who share your view in this affair. You will raise your hands to heaven and woefully cry, "Truly because I have denied the Lord God has he brought this judgment upon me!"[3]

The letter terrified Theodosius. He revoked the laws favoring pagans and Jews, and in March 425 he dismissed Eudocia's uncle. This was a setback for Eudocia and the traditionalists, but with their help she initiated another activity that changed the face of the city.

Why Mary?

Eudocia used Theodosius's interest in literature and writing to convince him to let her reorganize and expand the university in Constantinople. She invited recognized scholars to teach the value of the Greek culture and to credit the emperor's success with his own classical education. Among these scholars was a former priest of the god Zeus who was reported to have killed Christians.

The popularity of these scholars infuriated Pulcheria. She saw the resulting Hellenization of the city as a threat to the Church. She also saw that the problem was directly attributable to the influence of Eudocia and Paulinus. They had intentionally limited her access to Theodosius. Without her oversight, he had become lax in affairs of state. She needed to find a way to get him to recognize the danger they presented.

On the occasion of Eudocia's birthday Pulcheria saw an opportunity. She sent Theodosius a contract to present a gift to Eudocia. As expected, the emperor signed the document without reading it. When Pulcheria arrived to secure the document from her brother, she showed him he had just signed a document giving his wife the "gift" of being sold into slavery! She severely chastised him for having fallen into the habit of not reading documents presented for his signature and reminded him of his responsibility as emperor. Eudocia and Paulinus had succeeded in limiting Pulcheria's access to her brother, but this event reminded him that her advice had made him the man he was. He would not forget that again.

Chapter 6

While Eudocia relished her control over Theodosius, Pulcheria built churches and chapels for the relics of saints, which were taken to Constantinople by those who had heard about her zeal for the Christian faith.¹ Unlike the Church of Saint Stephen, which was elaborate but inaccessible to the public, the churches and chapels Pulcheria built were constructed in areas where the people could be blessed by the relics. Pulcheria's idea was that the saints, through the presence of their relics, would dwell with the people. She spared no expense to ensure that the structures were lavish, befitting the saints they represented. Everything she did was done out of love for the Virgin Mary and a desire to emulate what the stories had said about Jesus' mother.²

Bishop Proclus used a sermon on the Resurrection of Jesus to praise Pulcheria for these structures built on behalf of the saints. He extolled, "When we see the trophies, there can be no doubt that the victory has been won. We wonder at the great soul of the empress, a brimming source of spiritual blessings for all."³

In 425, a religious man named Alexander arrived in the city with his followers, who were known as the "sleepless ones" due to their austerity and self-denial. Alexander spoke publicly against the emperor's recent actions, which appeared to undermine the Church. Because people revered these holy men, the authorities were reluctant to act against them. Some high-ranking religious leaders who enjoyed the favor of the authorities incited a mob against Alexander and his followers, who were forced to take refuge in the Church of the Apostles. Pulcheria learned that a monk named Hypatius was in danger and sent men to collect the names of the members of the mob.⁴ When the mobsters learned they had been targeted by Pulcheria, they fled. Pulcheria and her sisters went to check on the well-being of Hypatius, and the monk insisted on going out to meet them and blessed the princesses. Such was the love the monks had for her in spite of the divide that had previously existed between the Church and the civil authorities.

Report of this incident reached the palace. Theodosius was relieved to hear that Pulcheria had successfully ended the insurrection with no loss of life. Paulinus and the traditionalists were not pleased. They saw that Pulcheria still held power over government troops and the authorities of the Church.

At the end of 445, Pulcheria's enemies again saw evidence of how much love and respect the Church had for her. On December 26, Proclus instituted a memorial for the Virgin Mary to honor Pulcheria and her cortege of virgins.[5] His sermons on Mary had always been popular. Instituting this feast for Mary endeared him to the people and Pulcheria. It also elevated Pulcheria in the eyes and hearts of the people.

Archbishop Sisinnius was another staunch supporter of Pulcheria.[6] When he died on December 24, 427, she removed herself from any celebrations to mourn his passing. Theodosius was touched by her devotion to the bishop. He remembered the teaching of the old priest from his childhood and the harsh letter from the monk Simeon and was overcome with guilt. He determined that he would choose a replacement for the archbishop who would uphold the true teachings of the faith. Above all, he wanted to choose an archbishop who would please Pulcheria.

Theodosius had heard about a man who not only had a reputation for asceticism but was a charismatic orator. Nestorius[7] was also passionate about stamping out heretical teaching. In the emperor's mind, this man could take the place of Bishop Atticus who had been such an encouragement to Pulcheria.

The emperor did not discuss this selection with either empress. He sent a military guard to escort Nestorius to Constantinople to make clear to all that this was the man he'd chosen to oversee the Church.

When Nestorius was consecrated as archbishop of Constantinople on April 10, 428, he was embraced by a cheering crowd. That event would be the highlight of his career in Constantinople. Nestorius's zeal and oratorical skill could not compensate for his appalling lack of political proficiency.

Four days after being consecrated as bishop, Nestorius began a crusade to stamp out heresy. He ordered the closure of the church where the Arians worshipped. Arians believed that Jesus Christ was separate from, and subordinate to God, the Father; many of them were Germans who served in Theodosius's army, including some of his generals. The Germans were so intent on keeping Nestorius from taking their church that they set fire to it.

Word of the uprising came to Theodosius from his soldiers. He called Nestorius to the palace and asked him to restrain himself. He might as well have told the river to stop flowing.

Easter fell on April 15 that year. The head of the deacons informed Nestorius about Pulcheria's custom of entering the altar area to take Communion with the priests and her brother. When Pulcheria arrived at the altar, Nestorius refused to allow her to enter.

"Only priests may enter," he stated.

"Why?" replied the empress. "Have I not given birth to God?" She was referring to Atticus's description of her virginity that equated her with Mary.

Nestorius replied vehemently, "You? You have given birth to Satan!" With that, he drove her out of the church.[8]

To say Pulcheria was angry would be a gross understatement.

Chapter 7

Summoning Nestorius to Constantinople was like hitting a wasp's nest with a stick. Not only did he not know how to be politically correct, he did not care to learn how to change. The stories Theodosius heard about Nestorius's zeal for stamping out heresy did not begin to describe his passion for biblical truth in Christianity.

Right after Easter, the new bishop closed the circus and forbade mimes, dancers, and games in the streets. Monks and priests were ordered to cease all outside activities and to remain behind the walls of the church complex. Any priest who refused to comply was excommunicated. Pulcheria and her virgins were overwhelmed as they tried to minister to the poor and needy people who previously had been cared for by the priests.[1]

Some in the civilian government welcomed the reigning in of the Church. But many of the religious leaders fought back. Hypatius was appalled at the way Pulcheria had been treated. He removed Nestorius's name from the altar list of the Great Church so he would not be remembered in daily prayer.

Basil, a famous religious figure and former deacon of the Church in Antioch, interrupted Nestorius as he preached in the Great Church, condemning the archbishop's actions. Nestorius ordered him arrested, beaten, and exiled. The people rescued Basil and carried him to Saint Euphemia, one of the churches built by Pulcheria.[2] The actions of the people against Nestorius's authority did not dissuade him at all.

On May 30, 428, less than two months after he arrived in Constantinople, Nestorius preached a sermon against heretics. In it he said, "Give me an earth free of heretics, O Emperor, and I will give you heaven in return! Help me destroy the heretics, and I will help you destroy the Persians!"[3]

The praetorian prefect received a proclamation issued by Nestorius listing all the heresies he intended to stamp out. It included harsh penalties for anyone who did not comply. Punishment against those who failed to enforce this proclamation was strictly enforced. Many people, heretics and compassionate citizens alike, were killed.

Many applauded Nestorius's efforts. But it was not only heretics who needed to fear his fervor. Cyril, bishop of Alexandria, had failed to send the customary gifts representing blessings on the occasion of Nestorius's accession to the position of archbishop of Constantinople.[4] Nestorius remembered this omission when a group of Alexandrian clerics who opposed Cyril used a minor land dispute to condemn the bishop before Nestorius. Because this was a civil matter, Nestorius took it to Theodosius. However, the emperor believed that because Cyril was a bishop, it should be handled by Nestorius. Cyril realized that if he was taken before a Church tribunal, Nestorius would preside and exhibit his skill in oration and persuasion. Cyril knew that a tribunal would only give his adversary greater public acclaim. Failing to find many who would support him, and knowing Nestorius had the support of the emperor, Cyril sought help from the one person in the imperial household who hated Nestorius: Pulcheria.

Meanwhile, Nestorius suggested that the emperor announce a memorial celebration for the martyr, John Chrysostom, and hold it in the royal court. (This was the same Chrysostom who had been the enemy of the emperor's mother, although Theodosius had been too young to remember.) The celebration was scheduled for September 26, 428. Cyril remembered the conflict between Chrysostom and Pulcheria's mother and knew that this information would solidify his connection to the empress.[5]

The animosity that had begun when Nestorius had refused to let Pulcheria take communion with the priests on Easter had deepened considerably. Nestorius had ended women's participation in evening psalms and prayer, saying that being out at night led to promiscuity. His action was so reprehensible to the women of the city that Helena, the pious wife of an important politician, verbally attacked him from the women's section of the church during a homily.

Nestorius knew the great influence Pulcheria had had on the people, especially the women, of Constantinople. He believed he needed to "put women in their place." But he also realized he could not speak against

Why Mary?

Pulcheria publicly. Instead, he wrote and published an apologetic work, *Bazaar of Heracleides*, which implied that Pulcheria had enjoyed adulterous relations with numerous men. Publicly he refused to honor her as a bride of Christ in his prayers for the royal family. Although only the most educated read the apologia, the people noticed his exclusion of her in the prayers.[6]

Further insulting Pulcheria, Nestorius refused to dine with her and her sisters, as Bishop Sisinnius had done. He also removed her portrait as Mary from above the altar in the Great Church and her cloak from the altar itself.

His greatest affront to Pulcheria, in her eyes, came when he met with leaders of two theological factions to discuss whether Mary should be considered the mother of God, *Theotokos*, or the mother of Man. At its core was the theological debate about whether Jesus was both fully God and fully man. Nestorius suggested that referring to Mary as the mother of Christ, *Christokos*, was a reasonable and acceptable solution:[7] Christ exemplified the idea of fully God and fully man. Those who sought to retain the title of *Theotokos* saw this as a slight against Mary and informed Pulcheria about the meeting.[8]

Shortly afterward, Anastasius, Nestorius's domestic chaplain, preached a sermon in the Great Church: "Let no one call Mary *Theotokos*. She was a human being, and it is impossible that God was born of a human."[9]

The people were stunned. There was much discussion about the sermon among the people from serving staff to scholars. One prominent Greek scholar, Socrates, argued that since Mary gave birth to Christ, and Christ was known as God, these words seemed heretical. Pulcheria was enraged. To her, this took away from Mary's dignity.

In fact, Nestorius believed that the use of the title *Theotokos* attributed to what he saw as the excessive worship of Mary.[10] In his eyes, Pulcheria's devotion to the mother of Christ had led to Mary's near deification. To deify anyone other than the three members of the Trinity was the definition of heresy.

In the fall of 428, Nestorius preached a sermon titled "Has God a Mother?" In it he stated, "If so we may excuse paganism for giving mothers to its deities … No, Mary was not *Theotokos*. For that which is born of flesh is flesh. A creature did not bring forth Him who is uncreated; the Father did not beget by the Virgin a new God."[11]

Eusebius, one of the imperial officials, shouted out that God in the person of the divine Word had, indeed, undergone a "second birth" in the flesh of a woman.[12] That this statement refuted the fact that God in three persons is eternal—without beginning or end—did not enter the minds of the people. When Eusebius published a propaganda sheet branding Nestorius as a heretic, saying he denied Christ's divinity, Pulcheria was one of the first to embrace it.

Pulcheria invited Proclus, bishop of Cyzicus, to preach on the Sunday before Christmas, December 17, 428. Because Proclus had been ordained by Bishop Sisinnius, Nestorius's predecessor, he could not be forbidden to preach. As this festival honoring the Virgin Mary had been made part of the Church's official calendar, Proclus delivered a sermon on Mary using the title *Theotokos*. The congregation was composed predominantly of women from all sectors of society. Pulcheria, her sisters, and other ascetic women had seats of prominence. The opening of Proclus's sermon honored them as well as Mary.

> A virginal assembly, my brothers, calls the tongue today to fair speech, and the present feast promises benefits for those who have gathered. This is most fitting. For the object of this feast is purity. The mystery it celebrates is the boast of the whole race of women and the glory of the feminine, on her account who was at once mother and maiden. This coming together is lovely to see. For behold earth and sea attend the Virgin, the sea gently smoothing her billows for the passage of ships, the earth hurrying along the feet of the traveler. Let nature leap in delight, and women are honored. Let humankind dance with joy, and virgins win glory. For where sin is multiplied, Grace has abounded even more. It is the blessed Saint Mary who has brought us together.[13]

Proclus went on to preach a sermon that would be copied, translated, and widely distributed to those who followed Pulcheria's devotion for Mary. But that day, though the end of his sermon was met with thunderous applause, one voice rang out clearly in objection.

"It is not surprising," Nestorius began politely, "that you who love

Christ should applaud those who preach in honor of the blessed Mary, for the fact that she became the temple of our Lord's flesh exceeds everything else worthy of praise." Then his tone changed. "Whoever claims without qualification that God was born of Mary prostitutes the reputation of the faith. [The pagan will reply] 'a god who was born, died, and was buried, I cannot adore.'"¹⁴

The crowd erupted in protest, drowning out Nestorius' voice.

The battle between Archbishop Nestorius and Empress Pulcheria had erupted into a war. Pulcheria could not help but remember her mother's similar confrontation with Chrysostom. But she determined not to allow what she saw as superstitious nonsense frighten her as it had frightened Empress Eudoxia. "Holy Virgin Mary, *Theotokos*, protect and sustain me," she prayed. She believed her destiny, originally to serve as protector of her brother, was now to protect the honor of the Virgin Mary.

In the early part of 429, Nestorius invited Bishop Dorotheus of Marcianopolis to preach at the Great Church. Dorotheus proclaimed that anyone who called Mary "Mother of God" (i.e., *Theotokos*) would be considered anathema.¹⁵

Pulcheria sent word to the people that they were welcome to join her in worship at a church near her residence, where they could hear "orthodox" statements on Mariology and Christology. Those who agreed with her theology of Mary but could not attend met in private residences.

It was not long before word spread about the theological war raging in Constantinople. Basil, a well-known and respected archimandrite from a nearby monastery, arrived at the archbishop's palace to try to find a peaceful solution. Nestorius had him beaten and turned over to the civil authorities, further inciting Pulcheria and her supporters. Representatives of Cyril, bishop of Alexandria, sent him copies of Nestorius's writings and sermons. Others sent copies to Celestine, bishop of Rome. Cyril sent letters of reproach to Nestorius, but they were ignored. Celestine contacted Cyril and asked for his opinion. Cyril responded with a long list of Nestorius's errors and a criticism of his theology.

The issue of the land dispute involving Cyril had evolved into a basis for the theological dispute. Cyril was afraid to go before Theodosius and accuse Nestorius of heresy, because he knew Theodosius and Eudoxia supported the archbishop of Constantinople. However, Cyril knew he had support from Celestine, who had indicated his support in his correspondence. More important, Cyril knew he could count on support from Empress Pulcheria.

Cyril composed three letters. One was addressed to Emperor Theodosius and Empress Eudocia. It praised the faith of the Theodosian dynasty and laid out orthodox Christological teaching and heresies, focusing on what he believed were the teachings of Nestorius. The second letter went to Pulcheria and her sisters, "the most pious princesses." This letter pleaded with them to intercede for him with their brother, the emperor. He supported his position with more than two hundred texts intended to refute Nestorius, and a list of bishops who had used the title Theotokos for Mary. A third letter was addressed directly to Pulcheria; it was by far the most scholarly of the three. He laid out principals of orthodox Christology that were intended to enable her to speak in theological terms when she addressed her brother on Cyril's behalf.[16]

While Cyril was writing his letters, Celestine composed one of his own. After consulting with his advisors, he sent a letter to Nestorius, to be delivered by Cyril. This letter told Nestorius that he had ten days to retract his "heretical" teachings publicly and to follow that up in writing to Rome. Failure to comply would be met with excommunication.[17]

Pulcheria had felt it necessary to avoid Nestorius. She loved her people, and she loved the Church and all that it represented. The conflict between her and Nestorius had caused a split in the Church and, worse, between her and Theodosius. When Cyril's letters arrived she believed they were a sign that she should go to her brother and try to forge a peaceful solution. After all, she thought, following the model of Constantine, was Theodosius not the emperor of the civilian government, and she the empress over the religious community?

Theodosius enthusiastically agreed to meet with his sister. He sorely missed her advice and encouragement. While he was loyal to Nestorius, he loved Pulcheria. She, in turn, longed for a restoration of their fellowship. Together they composed a letter, sent by his hand, from the imperial palace, convoking the Third Ecumenical Council. Theodosius called for all metropolitan bishops and their associates to gather at Ephesus on Pentecost, June 7, 431. The letter expressly forbade any attempts to resolve the disagreements by any means until that time.[18]

By the time Cyril's bishops arrived to deliver Celestine's ultimatum to

Nestorius, it had already been rendered null by the emperor's own hand. This was thanks in part to Nestorius's suggestion to Theodosius, prior to Pulcheria's visit, that a council should be convened.

For those bishops called to attend the council, this was to be a Christological debate. Would council members uphold the Nicene Creed that stated Jesus was fully God and fully Man? Would they uphold or condemn Nestorius?

For Pulcheria, the calling of this council had only one real purpose: to remove her archenemy, Nestorius. His attacks on the women of Constantinople had been problematic. However, what she saw as his attack on the Virgin Mary was reprehensible. She firmly believed that she was a true representation of Mary. Had not Bishops Atticus and Proclus so stated in their sermons? Thus, any attack on the Virgin Mary was an attack on Pulcheria, and any attack on Pulcheria was viewed, by her at least, an attack on the mother of Jesus Christ.

While the logical place for the council was in Constantinople, Pulcheria convinced her brother to hold it in Ephesus. It was commonly known that Mary had lived there with the apostle John after Jesus placed her in John's care. It was the perfect location, in Pulcheria's estimation; the church in Ephesus was one of the first built in Mary's honor. If this was to be a battle for Mary's name, let it take place on Mary's turf!

Theodosius felt some guilt over shutting his sister out of his life. He still adored and respected her. He recalled how many times her advice had positively affected outcomes in civil and Church affairs. Yet, he still supported Nestorius. Agreeing to have the council convene in Ephesus in the church dedicated to Mary would appease Pulcheria. But he also believed that the council would support his archbishop and that his sister would accept whatever the council decided. He apparently did not fully realize how passionate she was concerning the outcome.

Pulcheria was adamant that the council uphold the title of *Theotokos* for Mary and reject the title of *Christokos*. When she met with Cyril, they discussed Nestorius's views and determined that the title *Christokos* meant that Nestorius did not believe Jesus was fully God. The rumor spread. Pulcheria realized that her brother would have the final word. She arranged to have messengers keep her apprised of events.

The theological battle that raged in Ephesus was fierce. By July 1, reports from both sides had reached the palace. Pulcheria had received her own reports and approached her brother to argue in favor of rejecting Nestorius. Many influential men in the city and in the military were enlisted in the battle against the archbishop of Constantinople; with Pulcheria, they urged Emperor Theodosius to banish Nestorius.

People of the city divided into factions and battled in the streets. By July 4, the anti-Nestorian group had occupied the Great Church. They refused to leave until the council's decree against Nestorius was publicly read and enforced. The next day they called loudly for their demands to be presented to the emperor. But their loudest shouts were for his sister.

> Many years to Pulcheria! She it is who has strengthened the faith! ... Many years to Pulcheria! Many years to the empress! Many years to Pulcheria! She has strengthened the faith! ... Many years to Pulcheria! Many years to the orthodox one!"[19]

The message Theodosius sent to the church did not resolve the issue. The decree against Nestorius was read, but it was accompanied by another that deposed Cyril. Negotiations raged on for another month. However, at the end of August, Nestorius lost the incentive to carry on, and Theodosius gave in. Though Theodosius had wanted the bishops to decide the issue, in the end, he made the defining determination.

Pulcheria was gracious to her brother. With her supporters she rejoiced. She celebrated the victory of the Virgin Mary over Nestorius. The people celebrated the victory of the virgin empress, Pulcheria.

On October 30, 431, Cyril, newly reinstated bishop of Alexandria, arrived in Constantinople and delivered a long letter, *Apology to the Emperor on the Correct Faith*.[20] The letter also addressed "the two empresses who appear to be one," a reference, of course, to Pulcheria and Eudocia. Pulcheria received it with grace and a clenched jaw. Eudocia had come between her and her brother. In Pulcheria's mind, Eudocia's interference could no longer be tolerated.

Chapter 8

Cyril's letter fanned the flames of the conflict between Pulcheria and her sister-in-law. In the letter he addressed Pulcheria as the one "who takes part in the care and administration of your empire." Eudocia was addressed as the one "who exults in the offspring you have prayed for" and "permits the hope that your dynasty will last forever."[1]

Eudocia was overcome with jealousy. The power grab she had so cunningly employed to alienate Pulcheria from the palace had proved to be fleeting. Eudocia had not given Theodosius an heir. The younger of the two daughters she had borne, Flacilla, had died earlier that year.[2] Pulcheria had convinced Theodosius that God's blessings of victory over enemies of the empire because of her vow of virginity—which Theodosius had proclaimed so publicly—would be greatly enhanced if he, too, were celibate. In desperation, Eudocia reached out to Pulcheria's sworn enemy, Paulinus.[3]

While Eudocia was frantically trying to restore her position with her husband, Pulcheria found herself with more power than she'd had since Nestorius arrived. The new archbishop of Constantinople, Maximian, was the recipient of her generosity and became an ally. He convened a synod of bishops to depose any bishop who refused to reject Nestorius. In response to her advice, Theodosius sent a letter to Cyril, asking him to tone down his doctrinal rhetoric that had become offensive to some of the more moderate bishops.[4]

Both Cyril and Maximian wrote to Pulcheria to enlist her help in convincing her brother to support their causes. Similar letters were sent to the powerful men and women in the city who openly supported Pulcheria's charitable programs. These secondary letters were accompanied by gifts of gold, peacocks, and decorative items befitting a wealthy household, intending to encourage them to plead their causes to Pulcheria.[5] The empress did, indeed, support their causes to a certain extent, but not because of the bribes. She longed to see unity restored to the Church. That goal surpassed any desire to appease any Church leader.

Maximian died on April 12, 434,[6] and Pulcheria, assisted by her trusted associate, Taurus, succeeded in having Proclus installed as archbishop of Constantinople. He supported Pulcheria's efforts to heal the rift in the Church. By the end of 435, seventeen bishops who had supported Nestorius had been deposed. Many suffered stiff penalties for resisting the pronouncements of the royal family: two were sent to the mines of Egypt; one to Petra; and Nestorius was exiled to the Great Oasis in the Egyptian desert. Pulcheria's efforts to secure the title of *Theotokos* for the Virgin Mary had been rewarded. More significant, Pulcheria's power and authority over her brother and the Church had been restored. But the balance of power was to shift yet again.

On October 29, 437, Eudocia's only surviving daughter was married to the emperor of the Western Roman Empire, Valentinian.[7] Before the wedding, the senator and former prefect Volusianus traveled to Constantinople to assist with arrangements. Because he was a pagan, he was accompanied by his devout niece, Melania, who resided in a convent on the Mount of Olives in Jerusalem. Volusianus and Melania were still in Constantinople in January 438 when he suddenly died. Melania remained in the city during the forty days of mourning. During that time she proved to be a peacemaker between the members of the royal family. When time came for her to return to Jerusalem, it was announced that Eudocia would accompany her to give thanks to God for her daughter's successful marriage.[8]

The truth was that Eudocia could no longer bear to be the outsider in the family. Once the wedding was over she had again been relegated to the sidelines. On January 28, 438, Theodosius and Pulcheria attended a celebration in the Church of the Apostles to welcome back the bones of John Chrysostom. It was clear to Eudocia that the exclusion was intended to show the joint authority of Theodosius and Pulcheria over matters of Church and state.[9] A few days later, Pulcheria encouraged Theodosius to issue another constitution against pagans and Jews. Enforcement of this law led to conflict between Christians and Jews, which, in turn, resulted in bloodshed. Pulcheria and Theodosius displayed a united front, calling for the punishment of the Jews involved.[10]

On September 25, 438, an earthquake struck Constantinople. Proclus led the people in prayer chanting, "Holy God, holy and mighty, holy and immortal, have mercy on us!" As he prayed, the quaking stopped. Pulcheria and Theodosius jointly issued a constitution calling for this hymn to be sung throughout the world.[11] Pulcheria continued to establish forms of worship, endorsed by the bishop who had so praised her years before. It appeared that the empress was again firmly in control. But Eudocia again intervened.

Eudocia's return to Constantinople in early 439 was met with a celebration due a holy woman of God.[12] Like Constantine's mother, she had prayed at the holiest sites. Like Pulcheria, she brought relics in the form of remains of Saint Stephen, the first Christian martyr. Having momentarily regained the love and attention of the people, she moved to have her ally, Chrysaphius, named imperial sword bearer and guardian of the sacred family. But she was unsuccessful in convincing Theodosius to send Pulcheria back to her own palace. Seeking advice from Chrysaphius, she then suggested to Theodosius that Pulcheria's holiness because of her vow of virginity was sullied by her involvement in civil affairs; she should be made a deaconess! Theodosius agreed, and ordered Proclus to perform the ordination.[13]

Proclus had long been a supporter of Pulcheria. He realized that ordination would strip her of power. He warned her in writing not to come into his presence. Pulcheria realized she had been outsmarted. Rather than causing uproar in the palace, Pulcheria moved outside the city to contemplate her future.[14] She was not lonely. Her many connections with powerful families and religious leaders urged her to return.

Theodosius had always been a weak ruler and with Pulcheria out of the way, Chrysaphius took advantage of his newfound power as the emperor's advisor. From 443 to 444, five members of Theodosius's court who had been loyal to Pulcheria suffered confiscation of property, exile, or execution. Eudocia began to fear him. She contacted her former ally, Paulinus. Because he was Theodosius's boyhood friend, she thought he might be able to intervene and alert Theodosius to Chrysaphius's hunger for power. She totally underestimated the depth of Chrysaphius's evil intent.

Chrysaphius charged Eudocia with adultery. He informed Theodosius that she had conspired with Paulinus to challenge and then assassinate the emperor and make Paulinus emperor in his place. Theodosius believed him. Eudocia was banished to Jerusalem and stripped of her imperial courtiers. The royal mint was ordered to stop producing coins with her image. Paulinus was banished to Cappadocia and later executed.[15] When Pulcheria heard what Chrysaphius had done she was not surprised. She was concerned, however, about her brother.

Pulcheria's concern for Theodosius was not unfounded. Chrysaphius certainly commanded much power over Emperor Theodosius because of his charismatic personality, but he was not acting independently. His godfather was Eutyches, a leader of monastic communities in Constantinople and the surrounding areas, who had lived a cloistered life for many years. When Eutyches emerged as a spiritual leader, he was deemed the "bishop of bishops."[16] Theodosius greatly admired the dedication and holiness Eutyches exemplified. Chrysaphius encouraged that admiration. Unfortunately, Eutyches, who had opposed Nestorius at the Council of Ephesus, now refused to confess the "two natures" of Christ. Even worse, he urged Chrysaphius to influence Theodosius to endorse his growing band of supporters.

Pulcheria had personally embraced the Formula of Union adopted by the Council in 433 as the solution to the question of the nature of Christ. It stated, "For there has been a union of two natures; wherefore we confess one Christ, one Son, One Lord." Whereas her spiritual heart was devoted to Mary, she knew that ultimately the true power resided in Christ. The matter of His true nature had a direct impact on Mary's rightful title, in her eyes, of *Theotokos*. She had actively lobbied for the Formula to be accepted. For her, its acceptance was a personal victory, and she believed the matter had been settled. However, now Eutyches, who believed Jesus was fully God and could not have had human flesh, was encouraging Theodosius to reconsider his position. She took this attack on the Formula of Union and Mary *Theotokos* personally.[17]

Bishop Proclus had been a staunch supporter of Pulcheria. When he died in 446, Flavian became archbishop of Constantinople. He was aware of the high regard in which his predecessor held Pulcheria. He also knew of her work with the local monasteries; the one Eutyches led was not one of them. Her reputation in the fight against Nestorius was common knowledge. Thus, when Eusebius, bishop of Dorylaeum, charged Eutyches with heresy at a local synod, Flavian recognized him as being one who had worked closely with Pulcheria in the Nestorian controversy.

Flavian ordered Eutyches to appear in the episcopal palace for a hearing. Eutyches failed to appear the first three times he was summoned. Finally, when he did appear, it was with an escort of the royal guard: Theodosius was making it clear that he supported Chrysaphius's godfather. The emperor's support proved to be no match for his sister's influence. On November 22, all the bishops present, as well as twenty-three archimandrites of Constantinople and its suburbs, voted to excommunicate and depose Eutyches.[18] Pulcheria celebrated this as a victory, but her jubilation was short-lived.

On March 30, 449, Theodosius issued an imperial letter calling for another general council to be held in Ephesus in August. One hundred fifty bishops again convened in the church dedicated to Mary, although the emperor forbade one of the most influential and educated theologians of the day, Theodoret, to attend. The bishops charged Eusebius and Flavian of adding the Formula to the definition of Christ and deposed them. Eutyches was restored to his position. Theodosius sent troops to enforce the ruling.[19]

One of the bishops in attendance was a representative of Leo, bishop of Rome. When Leo heard what had transpired he immediately sent word to Flavian that the See of Peter, which the Rome believed carried the full authority of Christ, supported the Formula of Union and that he would sent legates to Ephesus in confirmation. The same day he sent two similar letters. One went to the archimandrites of Constantinople. The other went to the Empress Pulcheria, whose reputation as a selfless defender of the faith had reached Rome.

> We have proof from many examples that God has established a great defense of His church in your clemency, and if the labors of priests have achieved anything in our time against the enemies of universal truth, it goes to your glory. For as you have learned from the Holy Spirit to do, you subordinate your potency in everything to Him by whose protection you reign.[20]

Leo encouraged Pulcheria to add to that glory by fighting against Eutyches's teaching "as is habitual for your piety." However, she did not receive this letter.

Four months later, on October 13, 449, Leo again wrote to Pulcheria. This time he commissioned her as "a special legate of the Blessed Apostle Peter" to intervene with her brother to propose a new council to meet in Italy.²¹ This letter also stated his support for the Formula.

Pulcheria was unable to intervene with Theodosius because Chrysaphius, who supported his godfather Eutyches, still held too much influence over the emperor.

Early in 450, Leo solicited letters from Licinia Eudoxia, Theodosius's daughter, her husband, Valentinian III, and her mother-in-law, Galla Placidia. The letters were sent to Theodosius asking him to act on behalf of the Formula and the orthodoxy of the Church. Galla Placidia also wrote to Pulcheria asking her to intercede with her brother.

The replies arrived in March. Chrysaphius had dictated Theodosius's responses: Flavian had been suitably punished. The truth was vindicated. The case was closed. Pulcheria's letter indicated her support but made it clear that there was little hope she would be able to exert any influence on her brother because of Chrysaphius.²²

Though Pulcheria's answer seemed hopeless, she was not. In prayer she sought God's protection, but also the intervention of Mary. Just as she had fought for Mary to be given the title *Theotokos*, she appealed for the Virgin to intercede for the honor of her Son and the truth of His two natures, human and divine, perfectly united in Him. Those who loved Pulcheria followed her example in praying to the Virgin Mary.

In addition to prayer, Pulcheria stayed apprised of affairs of state. She knew Chrysaphius had hired the Isaurian army to protect the city, assuring that he, rather than Theodosius, would have the upper hand over military power. This was done behind the back of the former Isaurian chieftain, Zeno, a pagan, who had been given authority over Theodosius's military by Chrysaphius as a reward for defending the city against Attila in 447.²³ This appointment of a pagan in place of General Aspar, a Christian and supporter of Pulcheria, had added to her hatred of Chrysaphius. When Pulcheria's extensive network of supporters informed her that Chrysaphius planned to turn a wealthy woman of Constantinople, one of Pulcheria's supporters, over to Attila as a peace offering, Pulcheria's anger reached a breaking point.

Pulcheria sent a message to Zeno offering her support in his efforts

Why Mary?

to overthrow Chrysaphius. Zeno responded and called for Theodosius to deliver Chrysaphius for punishment because he had circumvented Zeno's military authority. Pulcheria also reached out to her brother, speaking against the heretical faith of Chrysaphius and Eutyches.

Theodosius had been unhappy with himself for allowing Chrysaphius and Eutyches to separate him from his sister's wise counsel. Her appeal to him to return to orthodox faith reached him just as he was berating himself for turning against her. Her message telling of the violence Bishop Flavian had endured at the hands of these men, which had led to his death, enraged Theodosius. He had Chrysaphius exiled to a remote island and his wealth confiscated.

As soon as Pulcheria heard Chrysaphius was gone, she returned to the palace to assist her brother in cleaning up the mess Chrysaphius had made of the government. She ordered the dismissal of the pagan, Zeno, and reinstated General Aspar. By July of 450, the workings of the government and the church again had the stamp and blessing of her hand.[24]

Her relationship with her brother was loving and non-confrontational. As always, Theodosius knew that she held no resentment because of the way he had treated her. In his own heart, though, he bore some guilt.

On July 26, 450, Theodosius sought comfort from his own guilt by taking his favorite horse out hunting near the city. The horse was frightened by a snake and reared, throwing Theodosius to the ground. Theodosius gravely injured his back in the fall. Two days later, with his adoring sister by his side, Emperor Theodosius II died.[25]

Acting out of grief, Pulcheria wasted no time calling for the execution of Chrysaphius. Once that was accomplished, though, she realized she was in a very delicate position. Whereas it was true she enjoyed the love and support of both the people and the Church, it was also true that, as Romans, the powerful men would not allow a woman to rule for long.

Pulcheria sought the advice of General Aspar, who had a close associate named Marcian of Thrace. He did not have money or aristocratic title, but he was a Roman. Aspar also attested to Marcian's loyalty to the empire and to the Church. Most important to Pulcheria, he was willing to respect her vow of virginity.

Despite the efforts of some to undermine her authority by saying that she would finally have to give up her virginity, Pulcheria's vast network of support held. On November 25, 450, shortly after their wedding, Pulcheria crowned Marcian. The troops, under General Aspar, proclaimed him Augustus (emperor). In the Great Church, the people of Constantinople, along with the whole clergy and monks from the monasteries, shouted out in acclamation of Marcian and Pulcheria. Then the crowd cried out for justice for Flavian and punishment for Eutyches. Pulcheria was not concerned: she had already written to Pope Leo, bishop of Rome.[26]

In her letter, Pulcheria said that the new bishop of Constantinople, Anatolius, had willingly agreed to support Leo's writings confirming the two natures of Christ united. She also reported that the remains of Flavian had been returned to Constantinople and that all the bishops who had supported him had been recalled "by force of an imperial edict."

Following the example Constantine the Great had established as civil head of the Church, Pulcheria requested that Leo summon the Oriental bishops to attend a general council. The purpose of the council would be to give unassailable authority to the Formula of Union and thereby introduce peace and harmony into the eastern empire.

Leo wanted the council to meet in Italy, but Pulcheria, supported by Theodoret, bishop of Cyrrhus, and other Eastern bishops, urged Marcian to call for it to be held in Nicaea in September 451. That summer, as the bishops were making plans to attend, Marcian was called to lead the army against the Hun invasion. Soon after he left, Pulcheria received reports that Flavian's enemies planned to disrupt the council and were assembling for that purpose. She wrote to the governor of Nicea, instructing him to eject everyone—monks, clerics, and lay people—who had no clear reason to be in the city. Her directive was explicit: "If any one of the other troublemakers turns up among those present, either before Our Serenity arrives or thereafter, you will be severely punished."[26]

As summer wore on it became clear that it would be impossible for Marcian to travel all the way to Nicaea. Marcian did not believe it was wise to interrupt his military campaign in order to attend. Pulcheria was not certain the governor could keep the peace. She encouraged Marcian to call for the location of the council to be changed to Chalcedon, across the Bosporus River from Constantinople.

On October 8, 451, one hundred twenty bishops assembled in the Church of Saint Euphemia. Pulcheria chose this location for two reasons:

first, it was large enough to accommodate the gathering, and, second, she felt the female presence of Euphemia, in the form of her relics, would ensure the desired outcome.[27]

In an unprecedented move, Pulcheria also called for nineteen of the most powerful men of the city both past and present to sit before the bishops. These men were not just to observe. They would propose matters for discussion, guide the discourse, and call for votes, ensuring Pulcheria's agenda would be carried out.

During the sixteen sessions between October 8 and November 1, the assembly confirmed and wrote Pulcheria's ecclesiastical policy into canons. They expanded the Formula of Union, giving it an explanation. They also adopted canon 28, which gave Constantinople authority as the New Rome to create new metropolitans for Pontus, Asia, and Thrace.

Throughout the council, the bishops would break out in acclamation of Marcian and Pulcheria for their leadership: "The emperor believes thus! The Augusta believes thus! Thus we all believe!"[28] More than once they proclaimed Pulcheria before Marcian, officially approving her function in organizing and directing the general council and restoring unity to the empire against tradition that had forbidden a woman from openly exercising this authority.

On October 25, Pulcheria and Marcian appeared in the church for the formal adoption of the new definition of faith. Marcian was saluted as "New Constantine, New Paul, New David." The bishops' praise of Pulcheria was even more enthusiastic:

> Many years to the Augusta! You are the light of orthodoxy! Because of this there will be peace everywhere! Lord, protect those who bring the light of peace, those who lighten the world! ... God will protect her, for she inherited orthodoxy! God will guard the protectoress of the faith, the ever pious one! God will protect the pious one, the orthodox, she who raised against heretics! You have persecuted heretics! You persecuted Nestorius and Eutyches! ... Marcian is the New Constantine, Pulcheria the New Helena! You have shown the faith of Helena! You have shown the zeal of Helena! Your life is the security of all! Your faith is the glory of the churches![29]

Despite their acclamations, the bishops did not officially recognize this as Pulcheria's council. Nor would she have wanted them to do so. Throughout her life Pulcheria made certain that her brother, Theodosius, or her husband, Marcian, were the focal points of power in the government. Her work in the Church was always credited to the Virgin Mary.

In the last years of her life, Pulcheria expanded philanthropy for monks to the holy women who shared her passion for Mary but who had previously been overlooked by the Church. She continued to support the many churches for Mary and other saints she had commissioned.

Although Pope Leo prevailed upon Marcian and Pulcheria to remove canon 28, he did so while praising them, writing, "I recognize in the princes of our time not only imperial potency but also priestly learning." Such acclaim of a woman was rare in the Church.

When Pulcheria died in July 453, she ordered her personal wealth to be distributed to the poor. She was laid to rest in the mausoleum of Constantine, near her father's tomb. When Leo I followed Marcian as emperor, he wrote an account of her life, calling her blessed. With his wife, Verina, he constructed a chapel next to Pulcheria's Blachernai Church to house a costly chest believed to contain Mary's shroud. Above the altar where the chest rested, Leo and Verina commissioned a mosaic made of gold and precious stones depicting the Mary *Theotokos* flanked by themselves and their children. The inscription on the altar stated that their imperial authority rested in their reverence to *Theotokos*. Pulcheria's passion for Mary had an impact on the Catholic Church that continues to this day.

Part II

The Development of Marian Devotion: Pulcheria to Vatican II

Chapter 9

The first part of this book is a historically accurate dramatization of the impact Pulcheria had on the devotion to the Virgin Mary in the Church. Its purpose has been to help the reader see the powerful influence one very passionate person had on the development of the Catholic Church. The foundation of this influence was certainly Constantine's declaration that Christianity was the official religion of the world. Although we might look at this as a good thing, two factors show that this event perhaps did not have the best effect on the purity of biblical faith and practice.

The first factor is called syncretism, which is a combination of two systems of belief. In this case syncretism occurred because people who already had strong belief in gods and goddesses were required to believe in Christianity instead. Rather than give up their beliefs, they merely transferred the names and personalities of their deities to those of the Christian church. The book of Acts gives us some insight. In chapter 19, we read about Paul's work and teaching in the city of Ephesus. God richly blessed him there, enabling him to perform numerous miracles of healing. Because of this, many in Ephesus became followers of Jesus Christ. The Scripture makes it clear that the culture and community of Ephesus centered on the worship of the goddess Diana. When large numbers of people became Christians, they stopped buying silver idols of Diana, and the idol makers lost business. Demetrius, one of the most successful idol makers, spearheaded an effort to reclaim their market. He led a group to the colosseum, where they chanted, "Great is Diana of the Ephesians!" As people heard the commotion, many came and joined them. This celebration of the goddess soon became a riot against Christians, who were seen as disrupting the thing for which the city was best known—the goddess Diana. Paul had to flee for his life.

The rift between the citizens of Ephesus and the Christians continued. Later, when Mary came to reside in the city with Jesus' beloved disciple John, the idol makers, as wise businessmen do, found that they could make the image of the goddess with a baby on her lap and just rename it Mary and the infant Jesus. Now the Christians who had been used to having shrines in their homes could have them again! The idol makers were happy. The people were happy. Celebrations for Diana were merged with those for Mary, the mother of Jesus. The differences between Diana and Mary became blurred in the minds of many of the people. That is how syncretism works.

The syncretism that took place in Ephesus happened in other areas as well. One of the most prominent figures of worship in the world around the Mediterranean was the mother goddess, which traced its roots back to the earliest man. People saw in the mother goddess the assurance of healthy crops and new life in animals and people. The mother goddess fulfilled the deep-set desire for love and compassion, which were not available from male gods of war and power. The same syncretism that drew worshippers of Diana in Ephesus to seek these qualities in the mother of Jesus attracted mother goddess worshippers who sought to conform to Constantine's state religion. They found a suitable substitute in the person of Mary, the mother of Jesus, recognized by Christians as the Son of God.

Hilda Graef, author of the critically acclaimed book *Mary: A History of Doctrine and Devotion*, describes how, beginning with Paul, teachers of church doctrine emphasized there is only one God, incarnate in Jesus Christ, who tolerates no rivals, male or female. As Creator and Redeemer of the world, He stands alone. There is no room for any other god or goddess.[1] This is in keeping with the first commandments God gave to the people through Moses. However, it is human nature to hold onto beliefs people find useful and comforting. Mary filled the people's longing for a mother goddess.

The second factor that influenced the development of Marian veneration occurred as a reaction to false teaching about Jesus. The New Testament scriptures have many passages warning against "false teachers." Much of the false teaching, which came to be called Gnosticism, centered on the idea that Jesus was not a true human man. To counter this false teaching, church leaders talked about the birth of Jesus. The accounts of Jesus' birth in the Gospels made it clear that Mary was Jesus' true mother in every sense, except that she remained a virgin when Jesus was conceived.

The epistles are virtually silent about Mary. The earliest writings of the church, those of the apostolic fathers (so called because they were said to have had a personal connection with the apostles), are similarly silent. One exception is in the writing of Ignatius of Antioch, who wrote around 110, that Jesus' true birth was "out of Mary and out of God."

Two questionable sources from the end of the first century to the beginning of the second go into more detail about the birth of Jesus and add details about Mary that are not confirmed by Scripture. According to Graef, these apocryphal books, *The Ascension of Isaiah* and *Odes of Solomon*, were greatly influenced by the false teaching of the Gnostics. In them we see the earliest mention of the idea of the perpetual virginity of Mary (a standard belief of those who had worshipped the mother goddess). We also see the some of the thinking that later would become accepted as Catholic dogma. For example, in *The Ascension of Isaiah* (first century A.D.), a story is told of Mary being astonished at the birth of the child, Jesus. It also alleges that her womb remained unchanged; she appeared to be as intact as she was before His birth: a virgin.[2]

Odes of Solomon (70–125) shows early evidence of other ideas that found their way into Marian doctrine. The concepts of Mary giving birth without pain and not seeking the help of a midwife, Mary's free will, her power, and the first reference to Mary in relation to salvation are all present.[3] According to Graef, these traits later led to syncretistic merging of the person of Mary with the Egyptian goddess Isis, mother of Horus, and to the mystical devotion of Mary.[4] When embraced by Pulcheria, the obsessed empress, this mystical devotion had a profound impact on the rise of Marian devotion within the Catholic Church.

The beginning of the second century saw a return to more scriptural teaching. However, as the century progressed, there was a greater focus on the role of Mary and a reinforcement of the popular notions that she was without sin and a perpetual virgin. The *Apology of Aristides*, a Greek philosopher writing at the beginning of the second century, compares Christian faith to pagan fantasies by emphasizing Mary's virginity and her sinless role as a consequence of her son's divinity.[5] In his *Dialogue* with *Trypho*, Aristides's contemporary, Justin Martyr emphasizes Mary's virginity, as well as her place in the lineage of Abraham, insofar as these facts were important to the developing idea of Mary's role in the process of salvation. Justin connects Mary's virginity to the prophecy of the virgin birth in Isaiah 7:14. While he did not place much emphasis on Mary beyond the fact that she gave birth to Jesus, he was the first writer to envision a connection between Eve, the "mother of all living" (Genesis 3:20), and Mary, as the mother of those who would find new life in her son, Jesus Christ.[6]

Early Christians, especially those with mother goddess backgrounds, wanted to know more about Mary. The Scriptures did not say much about her. In the middle of the third century, this hunger was fed by a writing known as the *Protoevangelium of James* or the Infancy Gospel of James, which appeared to provide some additional details about Mary. In it she is said to have been an exceptional child whose birth to sterile parents had been foretold by an angel. The story says she was dedicated to God and reared in the temple from the age of three. While in the temple, Mary supposedly was given a prophecy, saying God would use her to bring redemption to the world. According to custom, when Mary reached puberty she could no longer remain in the temple, so a husband was chosen for her through a miracle similar to the miracle of Aaron's rod in the Old Testament. From this point in the narrative, the *Protoevangelium* coincides with the Gospel of Luke's account of the announcement to Mary by an angel that she had been chosen to be the mother of the promised Messiah. From here other stories about Mary are interwoven with the gospel account.[7]

The ultimate focus of this story was to underscore the idea that Mary was without sin and remained a virgin not only at the conception of Jesus but throughout the birthing process. It intended to depict her as a woman worthy to be the mother of the Messiah. Although all the major Catholic beliefs about Mary have basis in the *Protoevangelium*, it is not one of the apocryphal books that eventually were accepted by the Western Catholic Church. (However, it was accepted by some Eastern Orthodox and Oriental Orthodox churches). This is because it does not meet the standards for inclusion:

- Apostolic origin: attributed to or based on the preaching or teaching of the first-generation apostles or those close to them.

- **Universal acceptance**: recognized and acknowledged by all major Christian communities in the Mediterranean world by the end of the fourth century.
- **Liturgical use**: read publicly along with the Old Testament when early Christians gathered for the Lord's Supper (their weekly worship services).
- **Consistent message**: containing theological ideas compatible with other accepted Christian writings (including the divinity and humanity of Jesus).

Because virginity was such an important part of mother goddess worship, the ideas of Mary as sinless and a perpetual virgin were eagerly embraced by those reluctant to let go of their pagan religion. But such ideas were also eagerly embraced by other Christians who wanted to know more about the mother of Jesus than was provided in Scripture. This became the fundamental reason for the extent of the adoration the people had for Mary.

The traditions of goddess worship were fertile ground for the stories that led to Marian adoration. But these traditions were not the only factor that elevated Mary from the role she was given in the Scriptures to the place she now holds in the Catholic Church. From the time the church began at Pentecost, there were those who refused to believe that Jesus was both fully God and fully man. The false teaching that denied this fact was denounced in Scripture by the apostles John, Paul, and Peter. After they were gone, the battle raged on. One of the bitterest battles was fought against those who wanted to deny the true and complete humanity of Jesus. Much of the early writing of the church fathers was an effort to counteract these erroneous ideas.

Around 280, Origen entered the battle. In an effort to affirm Jesus' humanity, he focused on Mary as the source of His fleshly nature. He wrote:

> In the case of any man it is appropriate to say that he was born "by means of a woman," because before he was born of a woman he took his origin from a man. But Christ, whose flesh did not take its origin from a man's seed, is rightly said to have been "born of a woman."[8]

Having thus set forth the humanity of Jesus, Origen argued for the deity of Jesus by referring to Mary as the one who was the bearer of God, the *Theotokos*.

As we have seen, whenever Christianity was introduced into a culture where goddess worship had been practiced, there was a movement to combine pagan religion with Christianity. The idea of a goddess having a son is one of the central themes of goddess worship. When Origen wrote about Mary as *Theotokos* in support of the humanity of Jesus, many former pagans embraced this title because it fit with their long-held beliefs. Remember, before Constantine, Christianity was not widely practiced. This was due, in part, to the persecution of Christians.

Around the same time Origen was writing about Mary as the *Theotokos* in support of the humanity of Jesus, this title was also being used for her in Egypt, a place where goddess worship had been practiced for thousands of years. The primary goddess, Isis, had a son who represented all the pharaohs. Isis also was worshipped for her power, which enabled her to resurrect her husband from the dead. It is not surprising that the worship of Mary took hold there. For example, archaeologists have found a papyrus text of a prayer from about 250. This prayer calls on the *Theotokos* to save the petitioner from danger and to let him take refuge in her mercy. It also extols her purity and blessedness.[9] This is one of the earliest records of a prayer being made directly to Mary by the laity. It is significant because it represents the popular devotion to Mary, which played a major role in the later establishment of Marian dogma. While Origen supported Mary as the virginal and holy *Theotokos*, he did not promote the idea that she was sinless. In fact, this early church father, according to Graef's research, wrote of the need for Jesus to have died for Mary's sin, citing Romans 3:23: "For all have sinned and fall short of the glory of God." To Origen, this sin was the doubt Mary experienced at the cross; a fulfillment of the prophecy of Simeon: "a sword will pierce your heart also" (Luke 2:35).

A writing attributed to Athanasius (circa 296–373), titled *Letter to the Virgins*, most certainly was read by the young Pulcheria. This document sets forth the premise of Mary's virginal life as a model. Athanasius does not teach that Mary was sinless, which would make her an impossible model for anyone to copy. Rather he focuses on her as an example of one who led a life that was pleasing to God. In the letter, he suggests any girl who wants to remain a virgin should imitate Mary. The influence of the *Protoevangelium* is clearly seen in in Athanasius's description of Mary as a woman who kept to the house, reluctant to be seen in the street; focused all of her energy on good works, prayer, and reading the scriptures; avoided men; and kept herself pure. He describes Mary as guarding her words and thoughts and refusing to react in anger, engage in slander, or be argumentative (except in civic matters). Mary's humility is expressed as part of her virginal example.[11]

In addition to being influenced by popular extra-biblical writings about Mary, Pulcheria would have heard about other Marian beliefs embraced by people seeking a mother-goddess type of figure. This is not surprising. Many saw God, especially in the Old Testament, as an angry, punishing, vindictive God, much like the authoritarian human fathers of the time. How much sweeter to be able to take one's petitions to a mother figure and let her intercede. For Pulcheria, whose own mother died while she was still very young, believing prayers could be made to Mary would have been appealing. This is exactly what began to happen.

The idea of Mary as intercessor was undergirded by new ideas about Mary that proved to be very popular with the people. Early Greek and Latin theologians, such as Jerome and John Chrysostom, perpetuated the idea that Mary remained a virgin throughout her life. However Chrysostom and others agreed with Irenaeus that she was not without fault. As the debate about the true humanity of Jesus became more heated, so did the discussion about Mary's role. Late in the second century, Irenaeus made reference to the contrast between the disobedience of Eve and the obedience of Mary. This idea of an Eve-Mary connection became fertile ground for the subsequent growth of the popularity of Marian worship.[12]

Around this time, a new Gnostic influence entered Mariology. The Gnostics believed all flesh was sinful. They were considered heretics, because they did not believe Jesus was made of real flesh; they believed anything related to flesh was unclean. This idea was embraced by some who questioned how Mary could be the *Theotokos* if she bore the taint of original sin. The *Protoevangelium* had already suggested that Mary was different from other women. The next seemingly logical step was to determine how, if all flesh was unclean, the incarnation of God through Christ could be conceived and grow in an unclean womb. In effort to counter this, theological discussion moved decidedly in the direction of seeing the Virgin as sinless.

A decade before Pulcheria was born, a Syrian named Ephraim wrote hymns to be used in Marian devotion. While it has been thought he was the first to reference the idea that Mary was born without the taint of original sin (Immaculate Conception of Mary), Graef suggests this is a misreading of his writing. She does, however, point to Ephraim as the first to use image theology by calling Mary the bride of her son, another common theme in goddess worship.[13] His hymns were partly responsible for inspiring the hymns Pulcheria would later contract for worship of the Virgin Mary.

Greek theologians initiated the discussion of the idea of Mary's perpetual virginity, but Latin theologians were not far behind. Zeno, bishop of Verona (circa 363–72), believed Mary remained a virgin not only in a moral sense after the birth of Jesus but also in the physical sense; giving birth did not interrupt her physical virginity. Zeno held Mary up as a great example for virgins and monks.[14] In Rome, Jerome vigorously promoted the perpetual virginity of Mary in his treatise *On the Perpetual Virginity of Mary Against Helvidius* (circa 383). His work as a biblical scholar coupled with his devotion to Mary led Jerome to see Mary in Old Testament Scriptures. These passages had not been connected to Mary by earlier theologians. However his use of obscure passages—"a garden enclosed" (Song of Solomon 4:12); "the king's daughter full of glory" (Psalm 44:14); the woman who would encompass a man (Jeremiah 31:22)—opened the door to giving Mary a title and authority not given to her by the apostles in New Testament scripture.[15]

At the same time arguments were being made for the perpetual virginity of Mary, debate was occurring in the East and West regarding the issue of Mary and original sin. John Chrysostom supported the idea of Mary's perpetual virginity. He did not, however, hold to the idea that Mary was without sin. In fact, he believed that Mary was in need of salvation in kinship with all mankind. While the Greek church promoted Mary as *Theotokos*, the Latin church was more hesitant to do so. Ambrose of Milan (circa 337–397) wrote extensively about Mary but generally refrained from using the title Mater Dei (the Latin form of *Theotokos*). At the same time, he was reluctant to ascribe fault or sin to the mother of Christ. He reasoned that because Jesus received his humanity from His mother, which made Him truly one of us, He was also sinless. Thus if Mary had not been given God's preserving grace, Christ's humanity would have been tainted by original sin.¹⁶ Others later expounded on this idea, which led to the concept of Mary's Immaculate Conception.

It is easy to understand how the young empress Pulcheria was captivated by these stories and popular teaching. Mary was depicted as courageous, blessed, and adored, just as Pulcheria's own mother had been. Having lost her mother at such a young age, Pulcheria found a substitute in the mother of Christ.

She became consumed with the idea of Mary as a perpetual virgin. She lived in a society where men controlled everything, from the government to the church. Her mother was able to gain power and authority only because Pulcheria's father was an uncommonly weak ruler who admired his wife's strength. Pulcheria realized few men would have allowed their wives to entertain such freedom. She had tasted personal freedom because of her early relationship with her brother. To enter into an arranged marriage would compromise her position.

Even as a young child, Pulcheria was forward-thinking. From the story of Mary, she knew a husband had been chosen for Mary when she reached woman-hood (about age twelve). Pulcheria did not want that to be her fate. She also knew, from the teaching of the old priest, vows of celibacy were not new to the church. Even Jesus taught that some people were not capable of keeping a vow of celibacy (Matthew 19:11–12). Paul claimed to be living a celibate life when he wrote to the Corinthians and stated that both celibate and marital lifestyles were pleasing to God (1 Corinthians 7:1–16). By taking a vow of celibacy before the government leaders could choose a husband for her, the young empress was able to avoid being set aside. Choosing to embrace the idea of Mary as "ever-virgin," and thereby asking to be allowed to follow Mary's example, ensured that permission would be given. Clearly the *Protoevangelium* and other stories of its type had great influence on Pulcheria.

The failure of early theologians such as Irenaeus, bishop of Lyons (125–202) and Tertullian (155–240) to recognize or endorse these stories mattered little to Pulcheria. The people loved the stories. The people eagerly embraced them as part of their faith.

Pulcheria's insatiable curiosity about the Virgin Mary undoubtedly led her to seek all there was to know about her idol. Because the emperor adored his young daughter, he would have spared no expense to satisfy her request. The Christian faith was central to the kingdom. What more admirable thing could a child desire than to know more about the mother of the Savior?

When we look at Pulcheria's life, we see how greatly she was influenced by these writings and how her personality molded them into the tools for what she perceived to be her God-ordained role in the lives of her brother and of the Church. Certainly Pulcheria taught her sisters and others who chose a virginal life to follow the rules on virgins laid out in the writing of Athanasius. However, her role was quite different. She did not remain behind closed doors. She had the examples of her mother and grandmother as well—women of power and influence! Pulcheria took from Athanasius what she needed and evidently passed the letters along to her younger sister to teach to her followers.

Because of her position, intelligence, and powerfully persuasive personality, Pulcheria was able to draw these ideas and writings together and carry the adoration of Mary to the next level. She was also wise enough to use the precedents set up by Constantine to further her cause.

Chapter 10

Constantine set several precedents that, when implemented by Pulcheria, paved the way for worship of Mary to flourish. The process began with the conversion of Constantine to Christianity in 312. The following year, in conjunction with Licinius, he issued the Edict of Milan, which ended the persecution of Christians and effectively established Christianity as the state religion.[1] This edict did not have a direct impact on the emerging adoration of Mary. However, when Constantine later removed all government funding from pagan temples and discouraged worship of gods and goddesses, the people looked for substitutes for their former worship practice.

Though Constantine professed to be a Christian, he continued to practice rituals tied to emperor worship that had been followed for centuries. He believed these rituals belonged alongside the worship of God. By imperial decree, he established an annual celebration of reverence for the emperor, which was considered a civic rather than a religious celebration. However, it included a parade featuring Constantine's own image carrying the image of the patron goddess of the city of Constantinople. As this image passed his reviewing stand, he bowed to it, in effect bowing to himself and the goddess.[2] The people of the city followed his example. These actions were more in keeping with emperor worship than Christianity—another example of how hard it is for people to break with tradition.

Constantine's strategy to close pagan temples through non-support helped to solidify Christianity as the new state religion. But retaining the image of the goddess of the city, the one held in the hand of the image of Constantine, showed his adherence to the tradition. He set up a new shrine for this goddess, hailed as the protector of Constantinople, across from the temple of Rhea, the guardian goddess of New Rome. Later, he set up a statue of his own mother and set the area aside as a shrine. In doing so he reinforced the idea of Rhea as "mother of the gods" in the mind of the people who eagerly embraced her.³ While their former pagan practices were no longer permitted, they were able to embrace so-called civil celebrations for this mother goddess. This became the foundation that Pulcheria eventually built upon to elevate the Virgin Mary to the place of the mother goddess.

While Constantine's reverence for goddesses certainly laid the stage for Pulcheria's later reverence for Mary, another of his actions gave her the authority to act. Constantine believed that he had been ordained by God to function alongside the bishops of the Church. He believed that just as they had authority to stand for true doctrine within the Church, he had authority to stand for doctrine as it related to the state. As a bishop, he called the first Ecumenical Council at Nicaea to address a key controversy within the church concerning the humanity of Jesus. This action later opened the door for Pulcheria to involve herself in church affairs.

As you will recall, Pulcheria felt justified in confronting Nestorius in his effort to clarify Mary's role as the mother of Jesus in His humanity rather than as *Theotokos*, the mother of God. This would appear to be a matter of language. But to Nestorius it was more than that. In his opinion, referring to Mary as mother of God was inaccurate: God existed before creation and has no mother. His apparent concern was that the title mother of God elevated her position to that of perceived deity, especially in the thinking of former goddess worshippers. When we look at Mary's role in the Catholic Church today, we see his concern was not unfounded.

Another powerful way in which Constantine influenced Pulcheria was in the realm of building churches. Constantine either commissioned or personally supervised the building of churches throughout his kingdom. In addition to changing Constantinople from a small town into a major city and the seat of his kingdom, he commissioned several churches there. Hagia Eirene, Hagia Sophia, and Hagia Dynamis celebrated the attributes of God—peace, wisdom, and power. On the site of the temple of goddess Aphrodite, he built the Church of the Apostles. In Rome, he built the Lateran Basilica, dedicated to Jesus the Savior; the Church of the Holy Cross of Jerusalem; and the original Saint Peter's Basilica over the site of the apostle's resting place. In Jerusalem, Constantine took personal interest in the construction of the Church of the Holy Sepulcher in the place traditionally held to be the burial and resurrection site of Jesus Christ. He also built churches in Nicomedia, Tier, Ostia, and Naples.

In addition to his own projects, Constantine entrusted to his mother all the assets of the treasury to support her efforts to glorify God through her own building projects. Helena oversaw the construction of the Church of the Nativity in Bethlehem and the Church of the Ascension on the Mount of Olives. She also helped her son select the site for the Church of the Holy Sepulcher.

While Constantine's churches were built to glorify God and the work of Jesus Christ and His apostles, the churches Pulcheria built later were dedicated primarily to the Virgin Mary. This was in keeping with her spiritual focus. During Pulcheria's lifetime, a church in Ephesus was dedicated to Mary. It originally had been a pagan temple known as the Hall of Muses. The date of its conversion to the church honoring Mary is not recorded. However, we know it was later than Constantine.[4] The Council of Ephesus, convened by Theodosius II, met in this church. This council pitted supporters of Pulcheria and Nestorius against each other regarding the use of the title *Theotokos* for Mary.

We have seen how Pulcheria would have been influenced by early writings and popular beliefs about Mary that had their foundation in goddess worship. We have also seen how she used precedents established by Constantine to influence the Church. But these were not the only things that influenced Pulcheria. Her own family history played a large part in her beliefs and actions regarding Mary, the mother of Jesus Christ.

Chapter 11

Pulcheria most certainly knew her family's illustrious history, where she found powerful men and women to emulate. These not only were figures of great civic and Church power, but also people of humility and compassion—passionate about their respective causes.

Pulcheria's Grandparents

Pulcheria's grandfather was Theodosius I (347–395). Known as Theodosius the Great, he became emperor of both the eastern and western parts of the Roman Empire in 379. One of his first acts after entering Constantinople was to issue an edict requiring all citizens to embrace the Nicene Creed that proclaimed that Jesus Christ is "the Son of God, begotten of the Father [the only-begotten; that is, of the essence of the Father, God of God,] Light of Light, very God of very God, begotten, not made, being of one substance with the Father." When the Patriarch Demophilis refused to conform to this creed, Theodosius had him expelled.[1] Six months later Theodosius convened the Council of Constantinople in Hagia Irene. This Council established five points:

- The Nicene Creed was confirmed with additions.
- The Holy Spirit was confirmed as equal to the Father and Son in the Trinity.
- The bishop of Constantinople was declared head over all other bishops except the bishop of Rome.
- Gregory of Nazianzus was confirmed as bishop of Constantinople.
- Constantinople was confirmed as the New Rome.

Three years later, Theodosius set a new precedent by naming his six-year-old son, Arcadius, Augustus and co-ruler of the eastern half of the kingdom. This action took place in the chapel, in keeping with Constantine's precedent establishing emperors as heads of the Church. The same year, the wife of Theodosius, Aelia Flavia Flacilla, received the rank of Augusta; that appointment was made in a civil rather than a church setting.[2]

In 384, following the example of Constantine, Theodosius I called for the destruction of all pagan temples. While some were dismantled, others were transformed. The temple for the god Helios was donated to the Great Church; the temple of Artemis became a gambling den; the temple of Aphrodite became a carriage house and a house of prostitution.[3] However Theodosius also followed Constantine's non-Christian example by allowing a statue of himself to be paraded through the city and placed in the chapel. This statue bore the inscription "Second Helios."[4] The city also erected a column with spiral reliefs proclaiming Theodosius's victories. It was similar to Emperor Trajan's column in Rome. In September of 384, Flacilla bore Theodocius I a second son, Honorius, whose name reflected the honor the city had conferred on the Emperor.

The following year, an event occurred which would later have a profound impact on our Pulcheria. Theodosius I had a daughter, also named Pulcheria, who was adored by people all over the city. Their reaction to her death was recorded by Bishop Gregory, who said it seemed the whole world had rushed to a single place to express their grief. The people flooded the streets to see the procession of her golden bier from the palace to the chapel. The whole of the city wept and cried out from the pain and sorrow filling their hearts. Gregory called her "a new-sprung blossom, with shining petals not yet lifted from the bud."[5]

While women of the time were not generally given much recognition or power, the elevation of Flacilla to Augusta gave her much greater visibility. Coins of the era that bore her image show the "hand of God" resting on her head. When she died in 387, the eulogy given by Gregory of Nyssa described honorable characteristics that could later be seen in her granddaughter Pulcheria. Gregory lauded Flacilla's philanthropy, her humility (tending the sick personally), her zeal for the Church, and her role as pillar of the Church. He hailed her as equal to her husband in authority (like Helena, the mother of Constantine).[6]

Flacilla was honored by the Church. But two decisions made by Theodosius I put him in conflict with the Church, particularly Bishop Ambrose. In 388 Theodosius was charged with burning a synagogue, and in 391 he was chastised for massacring citizens who rioted in Thessalonica. In an unprecedented action of humility and obedience reflecting his deep faith in God, Theodosius made a public confession for these actions. He followed this confession with the passage of laws forbidding paganism. His next act, taking the head of John the Baptist to Constantinople,[7] later inspired Pulcheria to seek out relics for the churches she built.

In 393, Theodosius legislated the Christian holidays of Sunday, Easter, and Christmas (the latter two using dates already being celebrated as pagan ritual days). He also proclaimed his younger son, Honorius, Augustus of the Western Empire. As a result, when Theodosius the Great died in 395, the Roman Empire was split into two.

Pulcheria's Parents

Arcadius was born in Spain shortly before Theodosius I became emperor. Though he was named Augustus of the East by his father when he was six years old, the title remained ceremonial until he was eighteen. When the emperor died, Arcadius became emperor of the Eastern Roman Empire while his brother, Honorius, became emperor in the west. Because of Arcadius's young age, much of the governing of the Eastern Empire was done by a prefect, Flavius Rufinus. Rufinus held great power but also had many enemies because he tried to manipulate Arcadius, a young man with a weak personality. Rufinus had a daughter of marriageable age, and he wanted her to marry Arcadius. However, he was called away to attend to affairs of state in Antioch, and his plans were derailed. Eutropius, whose title was chief of the sacred household, had been an integral part of Arcadius's existence for all of the young emperor's life. Influenced by the wealthy, powerful citizen Promotus, Eutropius encouraged the impressionable emperor to consider Eudoxia as his bride. Receiving a positive reaction from Arcadius, Eutropius ordered the people of Constantinople to prepare themselves for a royal wedding. Rufinus returned to the city at the time of the wedding procession, but it was not until the procession stopped in front of Promotus's home and wedding gifts were given to Eudoxia that Rufinus realized his plans had been foiled. Arcadius and Eudoxia were married on April 27, 395.

Eudoxia fully embraced the image of an emperor's wife that had been extolled by Gregory of Nyssa in his eulogy for Flacilla. She set out to fulfill her duties as a wife quickly. She presented Arcadius with their first child, a girl, on June 17, 397. They named her Flacilla after her paternal grandmother. The emperor's second daughter was born on January 19, 399. She was named Pulcheria after Arcadius's dead sister, who had been so adored by the people. A third daughter, Arcadia, was born on April 3, 400. Just one year later, on April 10, 401, Eudoxia finally gave birth to a son and heir to Arcadius. He was named Theodosius II after his grandfather and was followed by another daughter, Mariana, on February 10, 403. Eudoxia died of a miscarriage on October 6, 404.[8]

Gregory had praised Empress Flacilla's piety, and in this Eudoxia also excelled. One of her first actions was to provide silver candlesticks in the shape of crosses to lead religious processions. Their purpose was to elevate orthodox processions until they rivaled and surpassed the pomp of events organized by the nonorthodox Arians in the suburbs of Constantinople. Eudoxia provided musicians and singers for the processions as well; they were actually her own household servants.

In 400, Eudoxia received an assembly of 400 holy men led by Porphyry, bishop of Gaza, and Mark the Deacon. They traveled to Constantinople to convince Arcadius to destroy the pagan temple of Zeus Marnas in Gaza. Arcadius had previously refused to do this, because he thought that if he allowed the destruction of this popular site, the people of Gaza would not pay their taxes. The assembly gained an audience with the empress through her servant Amantius, who was known as a "servant of God." Eudoxia was pregnant at the time. Porphyry blessed the child and promised the empress that God would bless her with a son if she intervened with her husband on their behalf. The entourage remained in Constantinople until the birth of Theodosius II.[9]

The child was christened on the Feast of the Epiphany, January 6, 402. As the procession left the church, Porphyry, following Eudoxia's suggestion, presented his petition to the infant. The priest who was carrying the child had also been instructed by Eudoxia. He raised the baby's head and decreed that whatever was in the petition would be granted. The assembly bowed before Theodosius to cheers from onlookers.

When Arcadius named his son Augustus of the Eastern Empire four days later, the people congratulated him on his son's wisdom. Arcadius, who had been repeatedly nagged by his wife, felt pressured to grant Porphyry's petition. Eudoxia directed her servant Amantius to find a zealous Christian to draft and execute the legislation.

After the temple of Zeus in Gaza was destroyed, Eudoxia provided the funds to build a church on the site and instructed that it be built in the shape of a cross. The provision included thirty-two columns of green Carystian marble from southern Greece which were enthusiastically received by the citizens of Gaza. When the church was dedicated on Easter, 407, Porphyry dedicated it in memory of Eudoxia.

Eudoxia's piety was further displayed when she played an instrumental role in moving the holy bones of martyrs from the Great Church in Constantinople to the Chapel of Saint Thomas in Drypia nine miles away. Eudoxia joined with the people of the city in the procession. John Chrysostom described the nighttime portion of the procession as a sea of fire as the candles and torches carried by the people were so numerous. Eudoxia was lauded by the bishop for her courage and perseverance; she had provided the linen that covered the box and personally carried the box for the entire distance. He described her as "the moon among the stars," because she laid aside her royal attire and donned a simple robe of the faithful. Chrysostom hailed Eudoxia as a schoolmistress for the people in her examples of zealous faith and humble spirit.[10]

Eudoxia's "humble spirit," so hailed by the bishop, cloaked not only a commanding presence but also manipulative personality. These qualities were at work in the circumstances surrounding Porphyry. However, they were in evidence even earlier. Arcadius had a trusted advisor in Eutropius. It was he who arranged for Arcadius to marry Eudoxia. Yet, by 399, it was clear Eutropius was hated by powerful men in both the Eastern and Western Empires. Eudoxia saw that this state of affairs might harm the popularity of her husband. In July 399, Eudoxia, with her two little daughters in tow (Pulcheria was nine months old), approached emperor Arcadius. With all three weeping and wailing, she told her husband Eutropius had threatened to send her and her children away. The emperor reacted just as she expected he would: he banished Eutropius immediately. Eutropius sought asylum in the church of Chrysostom, but the public outcry was so great he went into exile on Cyprus. Six months later, on January 9, 400, Emperor Arcadius elevated Eudoxia to the position of Augusta with the presentation of a purple robe and royal crown of signifying her status. Coins with her image were minted and, as they had with Empress Flacilla, showed the hand of God crowning Eudoxia with a wreath.[11]

When we look at Pulcheria's life we see her following her mother's example of piety and service. But we also see her mother's influence in one other powerful way: a willingness to engage in battle with a Church representative. For Eudoxia, this encounter was with John Chrysostom. He had received his education in Antioch, where he was trained to interpret Scripture in a strict, literal way following ancient custom. His preaching and teaching were so eloquent, he became known as "John the Golden Mouth." Chrysostom was unanimously selected, by both the episcopacy and the people of Constantinople, to be their bishop. When he arrived in the city, however, he realized the power the aristocracy held over the Church did not conform to what he had been taught about the structure of Church government.

Nevertheless, Chrysostom embraced his new position with fervor. In accordance with his schooling he wielded his authority over the local clergy through strict discipline. He also enthusiastically evangelized the Gothic population of the city. He viewed the recent growth of the monastic movement as a threat to the structure of Church authority. When a popular spiritual leader of a monastery near Constantinople took his monks into the city to help sick and homeless people, he was embraced by the populace as well as by the empress. When Chrysostom refused to support the monks in favor of his own charitable institutions, Eudoxia made sure the monks received support from the government.

We have seen how Chrysostom praised Eudoxia for her piety and humility in conjunction with her participation in the movement of relics from the city to a neighboring town. However, the praise he gave in this instance was an exception to his regular teaching. Chrysostom did not have a high opinion of women. He likened them to disobedient Eve and spoke of them as vain and malicious. In his opinion they were useful only for bearing children and managing household functions. He saw for women no place in authority, especially not in spiritual leadership, and warned they would, whenever possible, try to insert themselves into these positions. He appeared to have Eudoxia in mind.[12]

If Eudoxia was, in fact, the target of Chrysostom's rancor, she did not disappoint him. The monks remained in the city, functioning with her financial support. Before long, another charismatic spiritual leader arrived in the city. Severian, bishop of Gabala in Syria, hoped to find financial support. His charm and persuasiveness soon won him influential friends, and he was brought before Eudoxia, who was also captivated by him. Chrysostom saw through Severian's schemes and ordered him expelled from the city. When Eudoxia heard of it she gathered up her infant son, Theodosius II, and entered the Church of the Apostles. She went straight to the bishop and, placing the infant on his knees, begged him, for the child's sake, to end his conflict with Severian. Chrysostom realized he could do nothing but concede to the request of the empress. When Chrysostom later baptized Theodosius II, Severian was asked to be his godfather. This only deepened Chrysostom's resentment of Eudoxia.[13]

Though Chrysostom was resentful of Eudoxia, he was not totally repulsed by women. Those who possessed qualities of modesty and who were obedient to his authority found favor in his eyes. One of these was a widow and heiress to a great fortune. Olympias had been ordained as a deaconess in the Great Church by Chrysostom's predecessor. She willingly followed his advice. Among her holdings was a vineyard, where Eudoxia enjoyed gathering grapes. Eudoxia eventually claimed this vineyard for the crown, attesting that she was entitled to it under imperial law, because she had been using it. Chrysostom intervened on Olympias's behalf but was rebuffed. Not long afterward, he preached about Jezebel seizing the vineyard of Naboth (I Kings 21).[14] The allusion was not missed by Eudoxia. Her resentment toward Chrysostom grew.

Two situations involving Chrysostom and Empress Eudoxia brought them to a head-to-head battle. The first was the arrival in Constantinople of four monks known as the Tall Brothers. Though they were lauded for their piety, they had been excommunicated from the Church by Bishop Theophilus of Alexandria. Chrysostom knew the bishop had a reputation for being hot-headed, so after examining the monks, he wrote to Theophilus to get his side of the story. In the meantime, the Tall Brothers sought out the empress's assistance. She took the matter to her husband, Arcadius, who called Theophilus to appear at a synod.[15]

In the interim Chrysostom gave a sermon against women that was viewed as a clear attack on Eudoxia. As she had done previously, she reminded Arcadius that any attack on her was an attack on the royal family. By the time Bishop Theophilus arrived at Chalcedon, the throne was leveling charges against Chrysostom. The Church representatives who were to question him were reluctant to do so. However, they wrote a report to the emperor that mirrored what they knew he—and Eudoxia—wanted to hear: they recommended the removal of Chrysostom and called for him to be charged with slandering the empress and tried in civil court.[16]

When the people of Constantinople learned their beloved bishop was to be exiled, they were furious. When the soldiers came to take him away he preached one final sermon, saying that Jezebel was responsible for taking the head of John the Baptist. The allusion to him and Eudoxia was not missed. The people rioted in the streets for three days, during which the soldiers kept Chrysostom in seclusion. When things calmed down, the bishop of Constantinople quietly left the city.[17]

Then God appeared to intervene. Eudoxia's eldest daughter, Flacilla, died. Whether it was because of an accident or illness was not recorded. However, her death coincided with the time period in which the people were rioting in the streets. Believing this was God's wrath, Eudoxia feared for the lives of her other children. Eudoxia wrote to Chrysostom and begged him to return to the city. When the letter could not be delivered, she sent her own servants to find him and return him to the city with a royal escort. Because he could not take up residence in the church until the decision of the synod was reversed, Eudoxia gave him one of her palaces. To the delight of the people, he announced his intent to cooperate with the empress in the future and that they would work together in peace.[18]

The peace did not last long. A representative of the royal family erected a silver statue of the empress just south of the Great Church and in front of the senate. The placement of the statue was accompanied by much celebration and a carnival atmosphere. The appearance of such frivolous activity so near his beloved church infuriated Chrysostom. In typical fashion, he preached a sermon on Matthew 14:3–12, where Herodias asks for the head of John the Baptist on a platter. The people knew he was referring to the empress.

Why Mary?

At Eudoxia's request, Arcadius had Chrysostom confined to the palace and called for bishops who opposed Chrysostom to charge him with acting as bishop without proper authority. The Church was cut off from the throne. When Easter arrived on April 17, 404, a number of parishioners arrived at the church dressed in white to receive baptism. Government troops were there to stop them and, in the ensuing scuffle, many people were killed. The tragedy was repeated the following day. Rioting ensued, and someone set fire to the Great Church. This fire spread to the senate building and on to the palace. In effort to mollify the people, Arsacius was ordained to take Chrysostom's place. The people refused to accept him, and the riots spread to other cities.[19]

The enormity of the situation was not lost on Eudoxia. She loved the people and was devastated by the loss of lives. She was pregnant with yet another child and the stress of the pregnancy coupled with the emotional stress of the civil unrest took its toll. On October 2, 404, the city was struck by a violent hailstorm. Thinking it to be a sign of God's wrath, Eudoxia had a panic attack, which proved to be too much for her weakened condition. On October 6, 404, Eudoxia died from complications of a miscarriage.[20]

Historians do not speak about Eudoxia's actions during these last months beyond what is recorded here. However, any mother will quickly envision Eudoxia surrounding herself with her children in order to ensure their safety. She most certainly would have relied on her eldest living daughter to help her with the younger children. In typical motherly fashion, when she realized she was dying, she would have entrusted them to Pulcheria's care. The tragic loss of her mother at such a tender age left an indelible mark on the empress's daughter. The idea that her mother's death was precipitated because of a conflict between Eudoxia and the woman-hating bishop planted a seed in Pulcheria's heart that would change the whole structure of Church worship.

Chapter 12

Part 1 of this book provided a historically sound novella of the life of Pulcheria. The first section of Part 2 showed how the empress was influenced to become the person she was and how she developed her ideas about Mary. But Pulcheria's influence did not end with her life. Pulcheria's passion for the mother of Christ had a far-reaching impact. Her zeal, combined with the desire of the people for a mother goddess figure, fueled the flames of Marian devotion.

The most visible evidence of Pulcheria's influence on this devotion is the honor she was given upon her death. When Leo I became emperor, he composed a narrative of her actions and accomplishments, which was read when he placed a carved image of Pulcheria on her tomb. Leo and his wife, Verina, later constructed a chapel next to the Blachernai Church that Pulcheria had built. The chapel was designed to house what was believed to be the shroud of Mary, contained in an elaborate chest. Leo also commissioned a costly mosaic made of gold and precious stones to be inset above the altar. It depicted Mary as *Theotokos* surrounded by Theodosius II, his wife, Empress Eudoxia, and their living children. On the chest was an inscription that proclaimed that the reverence shown to Mary, mother of Jesus, by the royal family would ensure their rule.

In Constantine's day, the people entrusted the protection of their city and nation to the goddess of the city. After Pulcheria, the city of Constantinople looked to the Virgin Mary for protection, comfort and mediation. The people enthusiastically embraced Pulcheria's passion. Relics believed to be associated with the Virgin were brought into the city with much pomp and ceremonial procession, mirroring emperor worship. These items—her burial shroud, cincture, and an icon of her purportedly painted by Luke—were housed in churches Pulcheria had constructed in Mary's honor. The names of these churches depict aspects of Mary that Pulcheria embraced. At the Hodgetria, which means "She Who Points the Way," mosaics show Mary holding the infant Jesus (a typical mother goddess image) in her right arm while pointing to Him with her left hand. The Blachernae points to Mary's humbleness and humility. The Chalkoprateria celebrates the Annunciation.

In addition to the churches Pulcheria built in Constantinople, other churches dedicated to Mary were built in major cities and in important Marian sites throughout the fifth and sixth centuries. One of the earliest churches named for Mary was in Ephesus. The Council of Ephesus, which established *Theotokos* as Mary's official designation, was held at this church in 451.[1] When the great Hagia Sophia was completed by Emperor Justinian in 537, the decorative accents included a mosaic of the Virgin Mary. On one side of her is a depiction of Constantine presenting to her the city of Constantinople. On her other side, Justinian is seen presenting to her the Hagia Sophia. While the Virgin holds the Christ child on her lap, the eyes of Constantine and Justinian are clearly directed to the Virgin. Justinian is said to have built about ninety churches throughout the empire, many of which were dedicated to the *Theotokos*.

One of the most notable of the churches built during this time was the one dedicated to Maria Regina in Rome. Here, Mary was depicted as queen of heaven, further evidence of the merging of civil religion and the Church during the time of Pulcheria. Statues, icons, and other artistic renderings portrayed Mary as a queen (as was Pulcheria), with the infant Jesus on her lap.[2] Non-Christian festivals celebrated her as a goddess, and in some places such festivals were organized by Christians as well. In response to the escalating focus on Mary, the Church made the effort to clarify the biblical teaching that stated Mary was not equal to God. Church leaders emphasized that Mary was the best example of whom human beings could become.[3] However, the same human nature that drew the Israelites to make a golden calf at the foot of God's mountain, and later caused them to desire a king, ultimately prevailed: the people wanted Mary to have a position equal to the goddesses of old.

Pulcheria had proclaimed the presence of Marian relics represented Mary's own presence in the city. She established at least two weekly vigils in Mary's honor to be celebrated in the churches with all of the honors typically given to emperors, including processions and hymns. In so doing, Pulcheria, by virtue of her civil and ecclesiastical positions, succeeded in promoting the cult of Mary to the same status she, herself, enjoyed in the hearts of the people. When she claimed—during her confrontation with Nestorius—that her identity was a representation of the Virgin's, the identity of the *Theotokos* merged with the imperial power Pulcheria held as Augusta. This act was a great factor in the people coming to view Mary, the *Theotokos*, as divine.[4]

The building of churches dedicated to Mary and Pulcheria's identification with the Virgin Mary empowered the people to view Mary as the new mother goddess. But Pulcheria did one more thing that ensured the people's devotion would continue to grow long after she was gone. She commissioned formal hymns to be written to the *Theotokos* following the pattern of imperial panegyrics—songs of honor and praise. These eulogizing poems had specific guidelines and generally included three specific devices: metaphors for astral or celestial bodies, comparisons with gods or heroes, and the artistic and powerful use of paradox to provoke a sense of awe in the hearts of those who listened to or sang the hymns.[5] They had the dual purpose of praising the emperor (or, in this case, the *Theotokos*) and teaching the people how to relate to the one being praised with wonder and reverence. Constantine had implemented changes to the formula when he insisted on being called the "one chosen by God" rather than being worshipped as a god. However, because Constantine viewed himself as the civil bishop of the Church, the writing of the imperial panegyric honoring the emperor became a Church function, and the priests found themselves involved in the civil ceremonies. Pulcheria's activities to promote the cult of Mary merely solidified what began under Constantine.

As we have seen, it was in response to Nestorius that Pulcheria first enlisted the help of Proclus to promote Mary as the *Theotokos*. Proclus proved to be quite adept at the task. He wrote several panegyrics to be used in the Church as hymns, replacing the traditional psalm singing. His most famous hymn, "Chairetismoi" (Salutations to the Virgin), was written for Christmas. He used events recorded in the Gospel of Luke and wove them together with popular, non-Scriptural, stories about Mary to form metaphors similar to those used in the imperial panegyric.[6]

The opening line of the hymn, "Hail full of grace," is taken from the gospel of Luke 1:28. The angel Gabriel greets Mary with "Hail, Mary, full of grace. The Lord is with thee." But we see little from the accepted biblical text beyond this reference. The hymn (see appendix) is instead full of metaphors that point to ideas put forth in apocryphal texts. Mary's perpetual virginity is pointed to when she is referred to as "unreaped soil." There are several references to her as the mother of God: "unfailing net of the immutable Godhead," "unsustained bearer," "weaver of the crown" (a reference to her supposed role in forming the fully God/fully man nature of Christ), "house of holy fire," and "torch-bearing light." Relatively new ideas about Mary's role in salvation and the life of the believer can be seen in the phrases "the return for those who fled," "dispenser of joy," and "light brighter than the sun." Proclus's use of the celestial images of "light" and "sun" are typical for both imperial panegyrics and goddess worship.

Scholars agree about the importance of this hymn and also that another hymn had a greater influence on the growth of the cult of Mary. This is the Akathistos Hymn. Scholars date it to about the time of the Council at Ephesus, the occasion of Pulcheria's attack on Nestorius. Three things make it important. First, this hymn is the oldest continually performed hymn in the Eastern Orthodox Church and has also had great influence in the West. Second, it is the most popular Marian hymn among the laity. Third, it attributes powers and activities to Mary that Scripture attributes to God alone.[7] In this hymn we see many of the ideas that have become tradition and dogma in the Catholic Church—both regarding Mary's role in the process of salvation and her place in a person's spiritual life.

The Akathistos Hymn consists of twenty-four stanzas; two introductory stanzas appear to have been added at later dates. In the original Greek, the main section forms an acrostic; each line begins with the next letter of the alphabet. The first half of the hymn recounts Gospel stories (including one from the apocryphal gospel of Matthew.) The second section praises Christ as Savior while weaving the role of the *Theotokos* into the salvation process. After every two stanzas there is a refrain: "Hail unespoused Spouse" (alternate translation: "Hail, oh bride unwedded"). In *Mary: A History of Doctrine and Devotion*, Hilda Graef gives an excellent summary of the Akathistos as "a compendium of Byzantine Mariology." She writes:

Through Mary, joy shines forth and Adam's fall is made good; she is the source and principle of the doctrines concerning Christ, she is both the heavenly ladder by which God descended and the bridge that leads from earth to heaven. As she is the admiration of the angels, so she is the defeat of demons. She is also the propitiation of the whole world; the benevolence of God towards men as well as the confidence men have in God. She is the mouth of the Apostles and the invincible fortitude of martyrs, she extinguishes the flames of passion, she is the joy of all generations—"Hail unespoused Spouse!" ... she is the sea that has drowned the spiritual Pharaoh (i.e., the devil), the rock which has quenched men's thirst of life; she is the pillar of fire leading those in darkness, the land of promise from which flow milk and honey ... she is the flower of incorruption from which the type of the Resurrection shines forth and which represents the life of the angels, she is the space of him who is infinite, and so she is the door to the mystery which has reconciled opposites, virginity and childbirth, and has made good the transgression, opened paradise and become the key of Christ's kingdom. She is the receptacle of God's wisdom, who shows the philosophers to be unwise and who illumines the many with wisdom ... the intercessor ... the fortress of all who have recourse to her because the Maker of heaven and earth dwelt in her womb; she is the minister of divine goodness, for she has regenerated those who had been conceived in shame. She kindles the immaterial light, illuminating the mind ... ; she is the type of the font that takes away the filth of sin. All who hymn her childbirth praise her as the living Temple: she is the immovable tower of the Church, the unconquerable wall of the Kingdom, the healing of my body and the salvation of my soul—"Hail, unespoused Spouse, deliver all from every calamity and free all who call on you from the chastisement to come!"[8]

Graef cautions us to recognize this hymn as a liturgy of devotion written from the viewpoint of a passionate devotee of Mary. Thus, these are not to be considered theological statements. However, when we look closely at Catholic theology we see that many of these ideas have become an integral part of Catholic faith and practice. Pulcheria's passion was clearly contagious.

Chapter 13

Once Pulcheria opened the door to the popular devotion of Mary and the Church's greater focus on her, theologians began to place more emphasis on this new area of study. There is evidence that shows that the two feasts of Christ, which were part of the Christmas liturgy, became more focused on Mary in the early seventh century. These were the Purification (February 2) and the Annunciation (March 25). The Assumption (August 15) and Nativity of Mary (September 8), which were more closely tied to extra-biblical writings, followed later.

Constantine and the Theodosian emperors—though firm in their insistence the people should not worship false gods and goddesses—did not hesitate to have statues of themselves held in reverence. In similar fashion, one of the first acts tied to Pulcheria's zeal for the Virgin Mary was the painting of an image of the Virgin above the altar in the Great Church. (The artist used Pulcheria's face as a model.) We have seen how Pulcheria also was intent on collecting relics of the saints and housing them in her Marian churches and other chapels. It naturally followed that icons of the personages tied to these relics would become focal points for worship.

Emperor Leo II (ruled 717–41) was opposed to the veneration of icons,[1] which led to tension with Germanus, patriarch of Constantinople. Germanus staunchly defended the use of icons, particularly in relation to the Virgin Mary. He reflected Pulcheria's earlier zeal for the Virgin and referred to himself as Mary's slave. Graef credits him with reinforcing two ideas that emerged in the eighth century. First, he preached about the bodily assumption of Mary, which reinforced the idea of her as sinless. Second, he presented Mary as an intercessor for the faithful before her Son and as their refuge from the wrath of God.[2]

At the same time, Andrew of Crete, archbishop of Gortyna, was also expressing his deep devotion to Mary. While he was not as convinced as Germanus was about the idea that Mary had been taken bodily to heaven (the Assumption of Mary), he was the first to write about the Feast of the Conception of Mary, putting more focus on her than on her parents. (This feast originally had been celebrated as the Annunciation of Mary's Birth to Joachim and Anne.) As with earlier Marian traditions, these ideas had their roots in the extra-biblical writings of the late second and third centuries. Andrew held to the idea that Mary was born without the stain of original sin. However, he did not go so far as to suggest her immaculate conception.[3]

All of these ideas about Mary in the Eastern Church during the eighth century were united in the writing and preaching of John of Damascus (circa 676–749). In his homily on the nativity, he clearly stated his support of the ideas that Mary was born without the taint of original sin and to her place as the second Eve. In three homilies focused on Mary's assumption, he alluded to her perpetual virginity, her sinlessness, and her bodily presence in heaven. John referred to Mary as queen of heaven, mistress of the angels, and a spiritual Garden of Eden. Recognizing the tendency of the people to relate Mary to the mother goddess, Kybele, John emphasized Mary's humanity yet gave her a place at the throne of heaven through her assumption. His adoration of Mary is evidenced by the authority he gave her, which was not given to her in Scripture:

- Guide of the destinies of the faithful
- The one who pacifies passions
- Grantor of future blessedness
- Place where the Tree of Life is planted and judgment is annulled
- Fountain of health for the sick
- Defense against demons

John attributes to Mary the ability to be in all places at the same time, teaching she will come to dwell in the thoughts of the faithful. For those who zealously practice virtue she will prepare a place in them for the coming of her Son. We see in John's writings clear evidence of the apocryphal writings that so powerfully influenced Pulcheria as well as the influence of the hymns she had commissioned to honor the *Theotokos*.[4]

The Church in the East had the advantage of a relatively solid and uneventful civic environment. However, the development of the Church in the West was confronted by invasions of Germanic tribes, whose influences led to differences in how theologians viewed Mary. By the end of the seventh century, the West had heard that four Marian feasts had been implemented in the Eastern Church. Around the time Germanus and John of Damascus were writing their homilies to the Virgin and celebrating four Marian feasts in the East, a Benedictine monk in England named Bede (circa 673–735) was writing about Mary in a more sober and scriptural way. He rejected the writings that had so powerfully influenced Pulcheria's Mariology. Instead, he focused on her as an example of humility. While Bede did refer to Mary as Theotokos, he was careful to say she is the mother of God in regard to Christ's humanity; Christ's divinity is from His Father. So though Mary is truly the mother of God incarnate, Bede was careful not to give her divine status. In spite of his caution to hold to Scripture for his theology, however, Bede did take the unscriptural position of seeking the intercession of Mary in prayer.[5]

Theologians in Italy were greatly influenced by Greek monks who settled there. Prior to their arrival, Latin scholars had not written about the Virgin Mary in the terms being used in the West. The four Marian feasts were being celebrated by the mid-seventh century. They were defended by Ambrose Autpert. In his sermons on the Assumption, Autpert used the title queen of heaven for Mary, citing the fact that she had given birth to the King of Angels. In his sermon on Mary's nativity, he stated, "No man is saved except through you, Theotokos." He attributed to Mary's virtue the purification of the world, the opening of paradise, and the salvation of men's souls from hell. In many ways, Autpert's praise of Mary echoed the Akathistos Hymn. His prayers to Mary also mirrored Eastern teaching, as did his references to Mary as a personification of the Church. Aupert's sermons on the Purification depict Mary as the loving mother not only of the Christ Child but of His brothers, the faithful of the Church. Here, then we see the idea of Mary not only as a personification of the Church but the mother of the Church and thus mother of all the faithful. While Ambrose Autpert merged the Eastern idea of Mary as queen of heaven with the Western idea of Mary as mother of the Church, he drew the Eastern ideas from the teachings of the Greeks alone. He formally denounced the writings about Mary's childhood as unscriptural.[6]

There were theologians who, like Autpert and Bede, rejected the popular but nonbiblical writings that had inspired Pulcheria's passion. But once Pulcheria opened the door for this type of literature to enter into faith and practice through her own example, the people's passion for similar, seemingly spiritual writings began to influence their religious beliefs. One such literary source was the Greek legend of Theophilus, which was translated by Paul the Deacon, who served in the court of Charlemagne in the late eighth century. This translation, Graef points out, gave rise to the Faust saga that, because of its great popularity during the next centuries, would have a great impact on the growth of the belief in the influence of the Virgin Mary's intercessory prayer. Paul's Latin translation of this legend was also the source of another aspect of Mariology. In it, we see the first use of the term *mediatrix* for Mary. While this idea did not become commonplace until four hundred years later, the seed of it can be seen clearly here.[7]

The Eastern Church was primarily responsible for the growth of theology concerning Mary during the eighth century. However at the end of that century, we again see the influence of the West. The bishop of Constantinople during this time was Tarasius. Taking his ideas from the popular, but non-scriptural Gospel of Saint James, Tarasius preached sermons on Mary that lifted her far beyond the voice of Scripture. His Mary delivers Adam from the curse. His Mary is the salvation of mankind. His Mary is so pure that priests place the infant Mary in the Holy of Holies in the temple! This Mary is given the names Sun, Moon, Throne, Pearl, and Eden. His *Theotokos* is the very reflection of the Creator.[8]

The tenth century saw another leap for Marian theology in the West. The poems of John the Geometer reinforced the idea of Mary as queen of heaven. He gave her a royal attire of gold suitable to this position and placed her in heaven at the right hand of her Son. Because she was the mother who gave her Son to die, and suffered at the foot of the cross all of His pain in her own heart, so would she suffer for the sins of each one of her spiritual children. For the Geometer, Jesus suffered and died once, but Mary suffered a million times as she gave her son for the sins of the people. As such, John's poems suggest, her suffering adds to the effectiveness of the suffering of Christ. John refers to her as a second paraclete, equating her to the Holy Spirit, and co-redemptrix with her Son.[9]

Popular devotion to Mary continued to increase, fueled by popular literature and plays based on the Theophilus legend and the so-called Gospel of James as well as on increasing reports of visions of Mary and miracles attributed to her. Odo, abbot of Cluny, called Mary "the Mother of Mercy," a name by which a vision was said to have identified herself. A bishop of Utrecht was reportedly healed when the holy mother of God appeared to him, leaving behind the scent of roses. A Benedictine nun, Hroswitha of Gandersheim, wrote plays based on the legend and the James narrative. In them she hailed Mary as the One Hope of the World and the queen of heaven who alone reconciles sinners to her Son through her intercession. Gottschalk of Limburg carried this idea of Mary as intercessor one step further when he wrote that just as Mary was the conduit for Christ to come to man, so would she logically be the conduit for man to come to Christ.[10] This idea of logic associated with Marian theology ushered in the age of scholasticism.

Chapter 14

The twelfth century saw what Giovanni Miegge calls a "scientific evolution" of Mariology, particularly through the works of Anselm and Bernard of Clairvaux.[1] Anselm did not view Mary as sinless, but his high view of her, exhibited in his Marian prayers,[2] helped pave the way for that Catholic dogma to develop. One of those greatly influenced by Anselm was Eadmer. According to Graef, his treatise titled "On the Conception of the Blessed Virgin" (circa 1126) was the first document to clearly explain the idea of the Immaculate Conception of Mary.[3] This document was not immediately embraced. However, it did provide grounds for the Council of London (1139), with the approval of Rome, to institute the Feast of the Immaculate Conception into the Church's liturgical calendar.[4] Bernard of Clairvaux (1091–1153) opposed the inclusion of this feast in the Church calendar. He believed that it exceeded the bounds of Marian veneration and history as taught by the Magisterium of the Catholic Church.[5] Bernard acknowledged that the Church had given the Virgin Mary many titles that reflected her dignity. He called for the Church to honor her for the purity and holiness she exhibited in her life. In this manuscript he upheld many of the ideas that had become part of the cult of Mary throughout history. However, he rejected the idea that Mary had been conceived without sin. Instead, he supported the teaching of the Church that her sinless state was a special gift of grace given to her by God, while she was in the womb, so that she could bear the Christ. To his credit, Bernard concluded this teaching by reminding the people that all he had said about Mary was only for the sake of her son, Jesus, who alone destroyed sin and death and obtained for us righteousness and eternal life.[6] Though Bernard firmly established that only Jesus Christ is our salvation, we can clearly see how the seeds of the passion of Pulcheria for the Virgin Mary influenced theologians through the centuries.

Debate over the idea of Mary's sinlessness continued for the next seven hundred years. Thomas Aquinas addressed this issue in his "Commentary on Peter Lombard's Sentences" (1254–56). He suggested that Mary's sanctification took place after her incarnation but before her birth, and that after her birth God gave her ability not to sin.[7]

As popularity for Marian feast days grew among the laity, the debate continued between the Dominicans, represented by Thomas, and the Franciscans, particularly the Britons, William of Ware (1267–1300) and John Duns Scotus (1266–1308). The Dominicans held that the idea of the Immaculate Conception did not coincide with the idea of universal redemption taught in Scripture. Ware's position was that if it were possible for God to sanctify Mary in the womb, it would be possible—and fitting for the future mother of God—to be created without sin from the beginning.[8] Scotus, traditionally named Subtle Doctor and Marian Doctor, is recognized as promoting the strongest argument for the idea of the Immaculate Conception of Mary. He provided a solution to the problem of reconciling Mary's freedom from sin with her need for redemption as a daughter of Adam. He proposed the idea of the pre-redemption of Mary; that is, her redemption before her conception. Scotus suggested that for God to preserve Mary from sin was a greater redemption than for Him to allow her to fall into sin and then redeem her from it. The most perfect redemption Christ could offer His mother was preservation from original sin.[9]

By the thirteenth century, the seeds of the cult of Mary that were planted in the heart of the people, especially Pulcheria, by stories outside Scripture had become an integral part of Catholic faith and practice. In writing about this era, Graef tells us that by this time the idea of the sinless Mary was generally accepted by Catholic theologians. To conform to Scripture—"All have sinned and fall short of the glory of God" (Romans 3:23)—they held that Christ's work was concerned primarily with wiping out original sin and only secondarily with the cleansing of actual sin. By making this difference, which is not supported by Scripture, they were able to propose that Christ redeemed His mother from original sin before her conception and then gave her special grace to remain sinless throughout her life. That these ideas were not supported by the true and inerrant Word of God was of no consequence. The tradition of the Church was given equal weight. Thus, the idea of the Immaculate Conception of Mary, though rejected by the Dominicans, was embraced by the Franciscans, Carmelites, and Servites of Mary.

In 1269 the Franciscans began instructing the congregants to recite the Angelus prayer (in its primitive form). This practice eventually spread to the Dominicans. In 1327 Pope John XXII (1316–24) ordered the bells in Rome to be rung every day at six in the morning, noon, and six in the evening to remind the faithful to recite this prayer to Mary. The recitation of the Hail Mary has not changed much since ancient times. The prayer would be recited in the church led by the vicar (priest) and the people would respond.

> *Vicar*: The angel of the Lord declared unto Mary.
> *Response*: And she conceived of the Holy Spirit. Hail Mary, full of grace, the Lord is with thee; blessed are thou among women and blessed is the fruit of thy womb, Jesus. Holy Mary, Mother of God, pray for us sinners, now and at the hour of our death. Amen.
> *Vicar*: Behold the handmaid of the Lord.
> *Response*: Be it done to me according to your word. Hail Mary ...
> *Vicar*: And the Word was made flesh.
> *Response*: And dwelt among us. Hail Mary ...
> *Vicar*: Pray for us, O Holy Mother of God.
> *Response*: That we may be made worthy of the promises of Christ. Hail Mary ...[10]

The Servites had already established a ritual of prayer to Mary. As a result of this ritual, and the ritual recitation of the Angelus, prayers to Mary for help, healing, and blessing became commonplace.

To understand how these daily prayers and devotion touched, and still touch, the heart, it is helpful to hear from Irish poet Seamus Heaney (1939–2013), who described the personal impact of his mother's devotion to the Virgin on his own faith:

> My sensibility was formed by the dolorous murmurings of the rosary, and the generally Marian quality of devotion. The reality that was addressed was maternal, and the posture was one of supplication ... The attitude to life that was inculcated to me—not by priests, but by the active, lived thing of prayers and so on, in my house and through my mother—was really patience ... In practice, the shrines, the rosary beads, all the devotions, were centered towards a feminine presence, which I think was terrific for the sensibility. I think that "Hail Mary" is more of a poem than the "Our Father" [the Lord's Prayer]. "Our Father" is between chaps [men], but there is something faintly amorous about the "Hail Mary."[11]

When one considers the addition of these prayers to the already common practice of erecting statues to the Virgin and other saints in churches dedicated to Mary, it begins to become clear how the Marian cult grew to such prominence.

The end of the fourteenth century was a time of upheaval for both Church and state. The Catholic Church was torn by disagreements over the identity of the true pope. Meanwhile, John Wycliffe, a seminary professor at Oxford in England, was calling for rebellion and biblical reform. Italy's city states were at war against each other, and France and England were locked into what would be called the Hundred Years' War. In the midst of all of this uncertainty, and without the safeguards of consistent theology, mysticism flourished. Bridget, a member of the Franciscan order, promoted Mary's place in the redemption of mankind by claiming to speak with the voices of Christ and His mother, Mary. Her writing referred to Mary as savior and implied that it is through Mary that all grace is dispensed. The latter concept eventually became part of the teaching of the Church.[12]

During this time, lay people lived out their devotion to the Virgin Mary. They prayed to the Virgin for healing and help with the many problems and sorrows in their lives. They made pilgrimages to shrines that had been erected to her. They asked her to intercede with her Son regarding their sins and knelt before her image in churches. They were unaware that there was an ongoing debate over the idea of the Immaculate Conception: they simply believed what they had been taught.

In theological circles, however, the debate raged on. Those who taught what was considered heretical doctrine were condemned and excommunicated. The chancellor of the University of Paris, John Gerson, was devoted to the Virgin but pointed out the multitude of theological errors that could arise if one held to the idea of the Immaculate Conception. Nevertheless, he credited Mary with the titles of Mother of the Eucharist, and Mother of Good Grace and invoked her presence at the Council of Constance (1414–18), which was convened to heal the schism in the Church.[13]

The Council of Basle was convened in 1431 in part to decide the issue of the Immaculate Conception. As they had in the past, the Dominicans opposed the doctrine while the Franciscans supported it. No decision was reached until after the council ended, so the decree that was issued approving the feast and the doctrine were not considered valid.

In 1438, the Council of Basle declared it was in favor of the Feast of the Immaculate Conception but did not have the authority to declare it dogma.[14] In spite of fierce objections by the Dominicans, headed by Juan de Torquemada (1388–1468), Pope Sixtus IV (1471–84) officially recognized the feast in 1480 by assigning indulgences to it. In 1483, Sixtus IV issued a bull, *Grave Nimis*, stating that as the Church had never ruled against the Immaculate Conception, no one could speak against it.[15]

The debate over the Immaculate Conception and its impact on Mary's place in the Economy of Salvation of the Catholic Church continued through the end of the fifteenth century.

Chapter 15

It is important to understand that from the time of Constantine to the Middle Ages, Christianity was at the center of much of the civilized world. Faith in God provided comfort and encouragement. Prayer was a daily—and for some hourly—activity. There was a general recognition that God was in control. However, three events in the fourteenth and fifteenth centuries caused people to see God in a different light: the Black Death, Hundred Years' War, and the Ottoman (Muslim) invasion of Europe.

The bubonic plague, called the Black Death (1346–53), killed an estimated 30 percent of the population of Europe. In many places, entire towns were wiped out. A large percentage of clergy called to minister to the afflicted died as well. As a result, many communities lost their most—and sometimes their only—educated citizens. In these places the desire for spiritual comfort was not diminished. While many people lost faith in God because their prayers for His mercy went unanswered, those who still believed wanted someone to lead them in prayer and worship. Often the person who stepped up to fulfill this need was unable to read Scripture; thus, he would preach what he knew or believed to be true, which spread false teaching regarding spiritual truth. In particular, such teaching reinforced ideas about Mary. She was viewed as a compassionate mother and contrasted with the angry God who had sent the plague.

The second factor to weaken the Catholic Church was the Hundred Years' War (1337–1453), a series of battles fought between the English and French to determine who would sit on the throne in France. It had an impact not only on civil government but also on the Church, as the two institutions were so closely intertwined.[1] The war changed that. On November 18, 1302, Pope Boniface issued a papal bull, *Unam Sanctum*, stating that the pope had authority over both the Church and kings. King Philip IV of France rejected this ruling and made an unsuccessful attempt to capture the pope. When Boniface died, Philip convinced the College of Cardinals to elect a French pope, hoping this would increase his military power over the English. Gregory IX was elected and moved to France. When Gregory died during a trip back to Rome, the Romans insisted that a Roman be his replacement. No Roman was qualified, so the cardinals elected Urban IV, a Neapolitan, to be pope. It wasn't long before they regretted their decision. Urban's temper and attempts to reform the Church made him unfit for the position. Most of the cardinals left Rome for France, where they elected Robert of Geneva (Clement VII) as pope. The existence of two popes threw the Church into turmoil, which contributed to a worsening of the ongoing war between France and England.

While the Hundred Years' War was weakening England and France, the Byzantine Empire in northern Europe was engaged in its own battles. Already weakened by the Great Schism in the Church that occurred after Roman crusaders attacked Constantinople in 1204, the empire was unable to withstand repeated invasions by the Ottoman Turks and eventually fell into their hands.

The split between the Eastern Orthodox and the Roman Catholics, combined with the split caused by the existence of the French and Roman popes, left the Church vulnerable to other schisms. People lost confidence in the authority of the Church. Debates over doctrine were no longer taken seriously because the problems of the world were so overwhelming. Stunned by the catastrophes that resulted from the plague and wars, people turned away from the Church. Instead, they sought solace in more human pleasures. This humanism was reflected in the Church as well. Graef notes that the hundred years that spanned the mid-fifteenth to the sixteenth centuries saw popes who not only supported humanism among the laity but also embraced the arts and human pleasures above religion. This was the age known as the Renaissance.

The Renaissance was like a longed-for rainstorm at the end of a drought. The ravages caused by plague and war left the people hungering for light, beauty, and the pleasures of life. Because they believed God had abandoned them, they abandoned God—specifically, the God of provision, hope, and answered prayers. The Renaissance began in Italy as developments in oil painting techniques made it possible for painters to capture realism in a way that inspired passion for their subjects. And just as the people of ancient times had desired to hold on to their goddess worship, during the Renaissance artists looked to God and the Church to find the subjects for their paintings. While the Virgin Mary was one of their favorite subjects, Leonardo da Vinci and Michelangelo used many other stories from Scripture to celebrate their genius. Oil paint and marble were expensive, but the Church was in a financial position to commission paintings and sculptures that brought biblical stories to life. However, it was humanistic life, not spiritual life, which captured the imagination of the people. Worship became objectified. Devotion for the Virgin and the saints, fueled by the proliferation of religious painting and sculpture, eclipsed biblical faith in God that had been lost during the Dark Ages.

The Renaissance also saw a resurgence of interest in intellectual arts. As more and more people were educated, they sought the writings of the ancient Greeks and scoured Italy for Latin texts. Writings about philosophy, natural thought, faith, and magic were equally valued. There was a revival of interest in science and math, and students learned the art of inductive reasoning. Colleges were formed and they turned out great thinkers, debaters, and writers. Because the Church had previously had the primary educational role, it is not surprising that monasteries became centers of learning.

Mary once again became a focus of the devotion of the people, even in the age of humanism. But that was about to be challenged. According to Graef, one of the great humanists of the age was Desiderius Erasmus of Rotterdam (1469–1536). Also considered by some to be one of the Renaissance's greatest scholars, Erasmus focused his research on the writings of classical Greek literature and the writings of the patristics. He is credited with laying the foundation of historical-critical thought through his study of the Greek New Testament.

When Erasmus was a young man, he had been devoted to Mary. His early writing refers to her as the ornament of heaven, and the one who shares the kingdom of heaven with her Son. In a prayer to Mary of Misfortune, he addresses her as the only one who can help in the calamities that befall man, the one who is invoked by all the earth.[2] Then he began to study the Bible and the writings of the earliest Christians. What he saw was a Church that no longer resembled the church of the book of Acts. The Catholic Church of his day was filled with superstition, abusive practices, and pious practices that were external, i.e., they did not extend to the hearts of the people. He recognized how far the religion of the Church, so focused on the Virgin Mary and the saints, had strayed from its original purpose. He wanted to see the Catholic Church return to Christ and moral law. To accomplish this purpose, he published *Popular Colloquies*, a group of essays that contain sharp criticism of the worship of Mary. One of these, "The Girls With No Interest In Marriage," includes a depiction of Pulcheria, though that was not his intent. "Pilgrimage" criticizes belief that the effectiveness of prayer to Mary can be enhanced by visits to particular shrines.

After visiting the shrine of Our Lady of Walsingham, Erasmus wrote an essay in the form of a letter from Mary. In this voice, he condemned those who prayed to Mary instead of her Son. The letter details the immorality of some of these prayers that reflect the abject morality of the time. Mary expresses distain for those who think singing hymns to her will garner them her favor and at the same time laments that they no longer recite the Hail Mary. To be fair to Erasmus, it must be noted that this essay ends with Mary warning against turning one's back on devotion to her completely. Though he strongly criticized the Marian devotion of his day, Erasmus was still a Roman Catholic.[3]

Erasmus's critical attitude toward Marian devotion can be directly traced to his study of original Greek manuscripts and the early church fathers. He rejected the concept of the sinless nature of Mary based on the rendering of the original Greek in the *Magnificat*. In the Latin Vulgate, the Greek *kecharitomene* was translated into the Latin *gratia plena*, which means "full of grace." Erasmus pointed out that the correct translation of *kecharitomene* is "favored one." He also corrects the translation of the the word "humility" to "lowliness," arguing that humility that recognizes its own value is not true humility. Erasmus argued against the idea that Jesus obeys His mother's direction in heaven, using the example of an earthly father who has no authority over a son who is a head of state. The criticism Erasmus levied against the Church regarding the worship of Mary focused on excesses of devotion to Mary by the people. Catholic scholars agree that Erasmus never truly left his orthodox faith.[4] However, his criticisms were valid and became fuel for the coming Protestant Reformation.

Like Erasmus, the early writings of Martin Luther (1483–1546) reflected a deep devotion to the Virgin Mary. As late as 1516, Luther was preaching sermons on the Immaculate Conception and the Assumption that mirrored Catholic teaching of his time. However, like Erasmus, Luther's thinking was changed as he began translating the Scriptures from the original Hebrew and Greek into German. Reading the Scriptures, Luther came to understand that the phrase "all have sinned and fall short of the glory of God" (Romans 3:23) included Mary. In his later writing Luther stresses that Mary was nothing, but that God had looked on her with favor borne out of His own grace and choice. Because of this, people could look to her as a model of hope. As she was nothing special, yet was chosen by God to be the one who bore the Christ Child, so can each of us, through God's power, bear the name of Christ to the world. To Luther, the idea of Mary bearing the Christ Child was no different from the cross that bore the Savior. Mary was human; the cross was wood. Neither had any more significance than that; nor were they due any greater honor. In 1522, Luther preached his "Sermon on Mary's Nativity," in which he said, "We are just as holy as she, for that she has greater grace is not due to her merit."[5] He added that if people never gave honor to the Virgin Mary, they would not be damned; but if they failed to recognize and help the poor, they would receive damnation.

While Luther equated the people's devotion to the Blessed Virgin with the cult of Baal, which was denounced by the prophet Jeremiah (Jeremiah 11:13), he did not do so out of any animosity toward Mary. Even when he spoke out against the practice of reciting the Ave Maria as a prayer, he acknowledged that Mary was "full of grace." However, this grace, he reaffirmed, was not due to who she was but to who God is. God's mercy and grace enabled her to be without sin at the moment of conception of the Christ Child. All of Luther's teaching regarding Mary was to move the focus of the people from Mary to Jesus Christ, her Son.[6]

Other reformers, although they differed in salvation theology to some extent, all held that while Mary was a good example of faith and humility, she should not be held in any higher esteem than any of the heroes of faith lauded by Scripture. John Calvin (1509–1564) taught that just as God entrusted Mary to bear the physical body of the Christ Child, He equally chooses Christians to bear Christ's name to the world. Ulrich

Zwingli (1484–1531) echoed the teaching of other reformers in teaching that intercessory prayers should be made not to Mary but to her Son; honoring Jesus Christ above all is the greatest honor one can give to His mother. Heinrich Bullinger (1504–1575) spoke of Mary as the example of a Christian filled with the Holy Spirit. All of the reformers had this in common: they were adamantly opposed to prayers being directed to Mary or the other saints. They adhered to Scripture and Christ's own words: "I am the Way, the Truth, and the Life. No man comes to the Father but through Me" (John 14:16).[7] Had Pulcheria been taught to love Jesus for the sacrifice He made on the cross for our sins and to seek Him only in prayer, she never would have led the people to devotion to His mother.

Our focus in discussing the reformers is to grasp the impact of their teaching in regard to devotion to Mary and prayers to her and the saints. However, the reformers also spoke out against other excesses of the Catholic Church, including the selling of indulgences (which people used as licenses to sin) and what they saw as corruption within the hierarchy of the Church. Foundationally, their attack centered on the theological principals of *sola scriptora* (authority of Scripture alone) and *sola fide* (justification by faith alone). The effects of the Reformation were far-reaching. The reformers' anti-authoritarian feelings about Church hierarchy became the seeds of resistance against the feudal system and the resulting growth of democracy around the world, as people embraced their freedom in Christ. It also gave rise to the anti-slavery and women's suffrage movements. The financial impact on the Catholic Church as people left her for the burgeoning denominations of the Protestant movement could not be overlooked. The teaching Magisterium of the Church recognized that there was validity in some of the reformers' charges. To correct these excesses and clarify the doctrines and dogma, Church leaders convened the Council of Trent (1546–1563).

The council issued issue two decrees that helped solidify Mary's place in Catholic faith and practice. First, during the fifteenth session (June 17, 1546), the council failed to include the Virgin Mary in its decree on original sin, effectively endorsing the Immaculate Conception. Second, in the twenty-second session (December 3–4, 1563), council members decreed that praying to saints to receive benefits from God through His Son, Jesus, was a good and acceptable practice.[8]

From this point on, the Catholic Church took a proactive stance in promoting devotion to the Virgin Mary and firmly establishing her place in the official teaching of the Economy of Salvation. In response to opposition to the idea of Mary's Immaculate Conception by Baius in 1567, Pope Pius V (1566–72) condemned the idea that her suffering was the result of original sin. The next century saw three popes—Paul V (1605–21), Gregory XV (1621–23), and Alexander VII (1655–67)—actively promoting this doctrine, although it had not been officially declared dogma.

While the Reformation advanced in northern Europe, Catholic countries continued to follow the traditions of the Church. The recitation of the Rosary in its current form was established during this time. The Feast of the Rosary was established by Pope Pius V, who credited the victory over the Ottoman armies at Lepanto to the recitation of the Rosary by the faithful in Rome.[9] The Jesuits, led by Peter Canisius (1521–1597), actively promoted the use of the Rosary to solidify the people's devotion to Mary and to the Catholic Church. Canisius's writing clearly laid out the beliefs of the Church regarding Mary. Though he did not recognize the validity of the *Protevangelium of James*, which had so captivated Pulcheria, he did state that the principles it described regarding Mary's Immaculate Conception, holy life, sinless nature, and perpetual virginity were all theologically logical and must certainly be accepted as such. Canisius's work was an apologia of Marian thought and practice but not a systematic elaboration of Marian doctrine. This, too, however, would be the work of a Jesuit.[10]

Francis Suarez (1548–1617) was a brilliant scholar. His work in international law and metaphysics, which extended to nearly twenty-six volumes in Latin, greatly influenced thinking in those areas during the next three hundred years. Suarez took his vows as a Jesuit at the age of eighteen and taught theology in various places until his death. He developed a systematic theology on the person of Mary in his treatise on the mysteries of the life of Christ. In his writing, the elevated view of Mary in the Economy of Salvation rises to even greater heights. His Mary has grace that exceeds the grace given to angels and men. In his Mariology, it is Mary, more than any other, whom Christ comes to redeem. Suarez credited to Mary merit that far surpasses that earned by all the saints combined. His Mary is a singular creature who holds complete theological wisdom and understanding concerning the Trinity, Redemption, and, in her knowledge of the Word, comprehensive knowledge of the universe and the state of all men, the blessed as well as the damned. Suarez embraces the idea of Mary as a contributor to the salvation of men on the basis of her own sacrifices; thus, reparatrix and mediatrix. These lofty ideas concerning the Virgin Mary have their foundation not in Scripture but in the traditions and beliefs that were nurtured by Pulcheria and grew through the succeeding twelve hundred years. It should be noted here that for all of this lofty language, Suarez was careful to point out, in deference to the charges of the reformers, that devotion to the Virgin Mary must not be the latria (worship) that belongs to God, alone, but veneration due her as mother of all men through her intercession on their behalf.[11]

Not all Jesuits held the same elevated view of Mary. Robert Bellarmine (1542–1621) was more cautious, seeking a middle ground between those who saw Mary as a goddess figure and the reformers who viewed her as equal to all of God's people. Bellarmine was also cautious about referring to Mary's Immaculate Conception: he rightly saw no basis for this idea in Scripture. In spite of his caution, Bellarmine did give to Mary the distinct privilege of being the one who dispenses all grace that originates with Christ: He is the head and she is the neck of the body of Christ, the church.[12]

We see in the writings of both Suarez and Bellarmine the influence of the reformers on Marian thought. The extreme devotion that had developed throughout the centuries was modified only a tiny bit in the writings of the Jesuits. This was not the case among the Franciscans. Lawrence of Brindisi (1559–1619) wrote that Christ and Mary were the same in nature, virtue, grace, and glory. To Lawrence, Mary was as similar to Christ as Eve was to Adam; thus, she was due the same worship due to God and Christ. She is given equal place with Christ in meriting the salvation of man; together, they confer remission of sin, resurrection of the body, and eternal life. Brindisi's description of Mary as the true wife of God is so far outside the teachings of Scripture that even Hilda Graef labels them blasphemous.[13] Yet, this is how far the cult of Mary had come in the thought and practice of much of the Catholic Church in the sixteenth century.

Chapter 16

Events linked to the Protestant Reformation in England had a profound influence on the decline of Marian devotion. Though the Augsburg Confession of 1530 (the Lutheran Church's founding document) did not specifically name Mary, it did forbid prayer invoking the intercession of saints. The Thirty-Nine Articles published by Elizabeth I of England in 1571, reaffirmed as Articles of Religion in 1662, more directly discouraged veneration of Mary. Article VI states that the sixty-six books of the Holy Scripture contain all that is necessary for faith and practice of the Christian life. The list of sixty-six books excludes those writings that were foundational in the development of the cult of Mary. Article XV affirms that Christ alone is without sin, effectively rejecting the traditions of the Immaculate Conception and sinless nature of Mary that had developed through the centuries. Article XXII rejects as repugnant to the Word of God (i.e., Jesus Christ) the adoration of relics and images and invocation of saints. This was intended to correct much of what Pulcheria had endorsed during her lifetime and had become integral to the faith and practice of the Catholic Church. This article also rejects as unscriptural the belief in purgatory and the practice of pardons (indulgences).[1] Had these foundational, Scriptural principals been taught to the young Pulcheria, it is likely she never would have adopted the beliefs that fueled the fires of Marian devotion for more than a thousand years.

The Age of Enlightenment, also known as the Age of Reason, had dawned. Dramatic progress in science, philosophy, society, and government from the mid-seventeenth through the eighteenth century laid the foundation for the modern era. As people's understanding of these areas grew, so did the belief that knowledge gave them control. Comprehension of man's life and destiny moved from God-centric to human-centric. Beginning with the French Revolution and the enthronement of the Goddess of Reason in Notre Dame Cathedral in Paris,[2] people began to throw off the hierarchal systems that had governed all aspects of their lives and replace them with political and social orders that were based on freedom and equality for all. The Catholic Church was not immune to the ravages of this upheaval, which began with the Protestant Reformation and spread throughout Europe.

By the end of the seventeenth century, the Catholic Church had reached a low point of influence. Its decline is mirrored in Mariology of the time. Even as the Age of Enlightenment led to a decline in Marian devotion by the laity, there was a movement to suppress it within the hierarchy of the Catholic Church. In many places, the Rosary was viewed as vain repetition that had been condemned by Scripture (Matthew 6:7 KJV), and recitation of it was forbidden.[3] There was a call to remove many Marian shrines. Some bishops removed scapulars, rosaries, and candles from the images of the Virgin in their churches. In 1773, Pope Clement XVI issued the *Dominus ac Redemptor*, suppressing the Jesuits, who were responsible for much of the teaching about Mary. Other Marian confraternities were also attacked. There were still pockets of Marian devotion among the laity, but sermons and tracts put out by congregations devoted to Mary were increasingly infected with superstitious ideas. The Holy Roman Emperor, Joseph II (1765—90), reinforced Constantine's idea of civil power over the Church and passed laws of reform and religious toleration that furthered weakened the Catholic Church. As the Church recognized Mary as its mother, devotion to her was weakened as well.

Much can be said in favor of the changes that occurred during the Age of Enlightenment. Certainly, it produced the seeds of thought that became the roots of individual freedom, the fruit of which was the Constitution of the United States of America. Yet, at the same time, the new focus on humanism turned many people away from God. The apostle Paul described this attitude: "Professing themselves to be wise they became fools, and changed the glory of the incorruptible God into an image made like corruptible man ..." (Romans 1:22–23). In seeking to control their lives through the knowledge of science, philosophy, and the natural world, people lost focus of the reality of God's omnipotence. At the same time the Age of Enlightenment was spreading from France throughout Europe, another form of enlightenment had begun.

The decline in Marian devotion spread, and many people abandoned the Catholic Church. Yet, faith in God and His Word grew and flourished in Europe. Popular writings of this time reflected a rejection of established religion and a return to Scripture as the foundation of Christian faith. John Milton, one of the most celebrated poets of this time, wrote *Paradise Lost* (1667) and *Paradise Gained* (1671), which focused on the relationship of the individual with God. Paul Bunyan's *Pilgrim's Progress*, which has been in print continuously since its initial publication in 1677, affirms the scriptural, personal relationship of sinful man with God; it was lost at the Fall but can be restored through faith in Christ. Bunyan emphasized that Jesus Christ is the only way to restore that relationship. Both authors make it clear that there is no intercessory role for Mary in the process of salvation.

Parallel to the Age of Enlightenment was the Great Awakening. The seeds were in the writings of Milton and Bunyan, but the water that caused it to grow was an outpouring of the Holy Spirit. The many ideas about humanism, God, and worship had severely divided a previously peaceful, God-fearing village in Germany. Nicholaus Von Zinzendorf, the nobleman who owned the land, was heartbroken and sought to restore peace and fellowship. He went to every home in the village and asked people to sign an agreement to live in harmony as brothers. A man prone to thinking in theological terms, he hoped to form a church where differing ideologies could worship together as a Lutheran congregation.

Shortly after Zinzendorf began his efforts to unify the community, he came across the constitution of a church that had existed in the area in the sixteenth century. This church pre-dated Lutheranism and its constitution was very similar to the agreement that he had proposed. On May 12, 1727, he presented this document to the people, who accepted it and dedicated their lives to serving God in community. On July 16, Zinzendorf poured out his soul to the people with tears. The people joined him in prayer for the community, and many dedicated themselves to doing so on a regular basis. On Sunday, August 10, a pastor named Rothe was overcome by the need to fall onto his knees in prayer for the people. The entire congregation felt the same compulsion and prostrated themselves in prayer with him. The praying, singing, and testimony continued until midnight and the bond of love among the people was solidified. When they came together for the Lord's Supper on Wednesday, singing turned to weeping and the powerful presence of the Holy Spirit electrified the entire assembly. The movement of the Spirit was so intense that the people could hardly describe it. Yet God was not done. On August 18, all of the schoolchildren were overcome by an outpouring of the Spirit and fell to their knees in prayer. Their prayer continued all night, and their lives were transformed.

The village sent out people to many different places in the world. Everywhere they went, a similar revival accompanied them. The Great Awakening spread throughout the world. England and America felt a special impact as the Spirit of God inspired men and women to proclaim the truth of the gospel of salvation through faith alone in Christ alone.

These great revivals at the turn of the nineteenth century turned many hearts back to God through faith in Jesus Christ as Lord and Savior. But it would take something else to draw people back to Mary. The superstition that had infiltrated Mariology throughout the centuries set the groundwork for the events of the Marian age to do just that.

Chapter 17

Visions of Mary were not peculiar to the nineteenth century. Popular literature of the late tenth century included accounts of three separate visions, by an abbot and two bishops in Cluny and Utrecht, of the Mother of Mercy, who was said to have the power to heal.[1] The cult of Our Lady of Guadalupe began with a vision of a beautiful lady who told a man called Juan Diego to tell the bishop to build a chapel for her at Tepeyac, Mexico. As with most visions, these were not formally recognized by the Church. In fact, the Catholic Church takes a very guarded stance regarding visions. However, visions of Mary, particularly those that occurred during the first part of the nineteenth century, drew the attention of people around the world. The appearance of these visions ushered in a century of unequaled growth in the veneration of Mary. In turn, the outpouring of devotion to Mary that accompanied the visions resulted in a renewed interest in persuading the Catholic Church to solidify traditional Marian thought into doctrine and dogma. The Immaculate Conception was the first teaching to be declared dogma during this time.

The first of the nineteenth-century visions was seen by a young woman, Catherine Laboure, who entered the convent of the Daughters of Charity of Saint Vincent de Paul in Paris as a novitiate (future nun). According to historical accounts, her passionate desire to see the Virgin Mary was rewarded: a young child dressed in white appeared on the night of July 19, 1830, and instructed Catherine to go to the chapel, where Mary awaited her. The chapel was empty and it was dark when she arrived, but all of the lights were on. After a time, Catherine heard "a rustle like that of a silk dress" and then saw Mary sitting in a chair by the altar. She reported that Mary gave her instructions about her conduct and explained other visions that Catherine had seen previously. In November, Catherine had a second vision of the woman, again accompanied by the rustle of silk. This vision, which appeared during her evening meditation, was of the Virgin dressed in white with a white veil standing on a white ball. A greenish-colored serpent with yellow specks was also there. Graef further describes Catherine's experience:

> The hands of the vision were lifted up, holding a golden ball surmounted by a small golden cross ... the vision had three rings on each of her fingers, adorned with wonderful stones which emitted brilliant rays. [Catherine] then heard a voice saying, "This ball which you see represents the whole world, particularly France, and every person in particular" ... the rays from the rings symbolized the graces Mary gave to all who asked her, while some stones, from which no rays went forth, were the graces men forgot to ask her for ... An oval frame appeared around the Virgin, inside which was written in gold letters, "O Mary, conceived without sin, pray for us who have recourse to you." The golden ball ... disappeared and the hands themselves remained outstretched, continuing to emit the rays, while a voice was heard telling Catherine to have a medal struck according to this model, which would obtain great graces for all those who wore it with confidence ... the picture seemed to turn round and show on the reverse side of the medal an "M" surmounted by a cross, and below it the two hearts of Jesus and Mary, one surrounded by a crown of thorns, the other pierced by a sword ... Mary told the sister that henceforth she would see her no more, but she would hear her voice in her prayers.[3]

The vision was reported to the Church and in 1832, with the permission of the archbishop of Paris, the medal was struck. It was distributed by Catholic missions all over the world. The medal became very popular among Catholics, and it was not long before there were reports of miracles being associated with it. The vision and the medal led to renewed interest in the idea of Mary's Immaculate Conception. Catholics began to call for the Church to define it solemnly as dogma.⁴

The growing popularity of Mary due to the vision spread beyond the Catholic Church. In 1832, John Henry Newman, a priest in the Church of England and a scholar at Oxford University, preached a sermon on the Annunciation in which he praised Mary's transcendent purity in such terms that he was accused of teaching the Immaculate Conception.⁵ His sermon represented a school of thought that would soon be called the Oxford Movement and would lead to a closer relationship between the Anglican and Catholic Churches. Newman converted to Catholicism about fourteen years after that sermon and eventually was elevated to the office of cardinal.

Pope Pius IX, a Marian devotee, took office in June 1846. In response to the growing public demand for an authoritative definition of the Immaculate Conception, he consulted the bishops. When he saw that only 56 of the 603 bishops were opposed to making a formal definition, he formed a special congregation to formulate the papal bull. On December 8, 1854, Pius IX issued *Ineffabilis Deus*, which proclaimed as dogma the Immaculate Conception of Mary. It read, in part, "The Most Holy Virgin Mary was, in the first moment of her conception, by a unique gift of grace and privilege of Almighty God, in view of the merits of Jesus Christ, the Redeemer of mankind, preserved free from all stain of original sin."⁶ This same document proclaimed Mary to be the mediatrix of all graces by virtue of her cooperation in the Incarnation and her intercession in heaven.

This papal bull went on to state "no one can come to the Father on high except through the Son, so almost in like manner, no one can come to Christ except through His Mother." Mary's authority to be mediatrix is tied to the idea that the suffering she endured when her Son died on the cross to atone for the sins of man effectively made her a participant in that sacrificial act. Therefore, it was decreed that her capacity to intercede for people was second only to the intercessory capacity of Christ. While the decree acknowledged that people are not obligated to ask Mary for grace, it did instruct that no one receives the redemptive grace of Christ without the intercessory cooperation of Mary. The Church understood that this pronouncement of the Immaculate Conception as dogma and the teaching that Mary is Mediatrix would be binding on all Catholics.

Gabriele Roschini, in his short catechism, provided an outline of the fundamental laws of the development of the Marian system in one primary and four secondary principles.[7] Roschini's primary principle affirms Mary as the Mother of God and the Mediatrix of man. The secondary principles of singularity, propriety, eminence, and analogy with Christ are developed from this primary principle. Roschini explained these four secondary principles as follows:

1. The most blessed Virgin being a creature altogether singular, constituting an order apart, rightly claims for herself privileges entirely singular which can fit no other creature (Principle of Singularity).
2. All perfections must be attributed to the most blessed Virgin which truly become the dignity of the Mother of God and Mediatrix of man, provided they have some basis in revelation and are not contrary to faith and reason (Principle of Propriety).
3. All the privileges of nature, grace and glory granted by God to the other saints must have been granted in some way also to the most blessed Virgin, Queen of the Saints (Principle of Eminence).
4. Privileges analogous to the various privileges of the humanity of Christ are possessed correspondingly by the most blessed Virgin and according to the condition of the one and the other (Principle of Analogy or likeness to Christ).[8]

In his catechism Roschini points out that once this dogma is established, it opens the door for Mary to be glorified to an even greater extent.

> The divine Maternity raises her to dizzying height and places her immediately after God in the vast scale of beings, causing her to be a member of the hypostatic order (in the measure that through her and in her the Word is united hypostatically—that is personally—with human nature), an order superior to the order of nature and grace and glory. For this the Fathers and the Scriptures have almost exhausted their resources of language in exalting her without succeeding in giving her the glory that becomes her. Her greatness borders on the infinite.[9]

As we have seen, this highly elevated view of Mary developed primarily through Church tradition. However, Marian scholars cite three passages as primary scriptural foundations for the dogma of the Immaculate Conception: Luke 1:28, Luke 1:42–43, and Genesis 3:15. While the Immaculate Conception of Mary is not explicitly stated in Scripture, Catholic theologians see it as implied in these and other passages. One of the keys to their interpretation is that the Latin Vulgate was used to provide the translation of these passages from the original Greek.

In the first Luke passage there are two statements that are primary to their argument. The first, and more important, is the Greek passive participle κεχαριτωμένη. The Vulgate translation renders this as "full of grace," which is further interpreted to mean that Mary not only received divine grace from God in compensation for original sin but was also preserved free from original sin from the moment of her conception. This interpretation views the angel's salutation "full of grace" as representing Mary's proper name and, thus, her characteristic quality. This idea of fullness of grace is seen as sinless perfection in her essence, not as a correction of any defect. Because Mary was chosen to be the mother of God (*Theotokos*), this essence of perfection had to extend throughout her life, beginning at her conception. This sinless perfection was necessary, they expound, because she was to give birth to sinless God. Thus, according to Ott, the argument is reasonably based on the scholastic axiom, "God could do it, He ought to do it, therefore He did it."[10] The second statement, that Mary is "blessed … among women," is repeated in Luke 1:42–43.

Luke 1:42–43 is the proclamation of Elizabeth. Scripture records that, filled with the Holy Spirit, she proclaims that Mary is blessed among women, and that the fruit of her womb is also blessed. Tertullian used this passage to argue against the Gnostics, affirming that Christ was fully man. Equating Mary to Isaiah's analogy of a root springing from Jesse (Isaiah 11:10), he developed the idea that the fruit (Jesus) and the vine (Mary) are of the same flesh.[11] Ott records that the idea of parallelism between Mary and Jesus suggested that Mary, like Christ, was sinless from conception.[12] Pelikan points out that while the title Lord (*kyrios*) in the phrase "mother of our Lord" can refer to Jesus, it is also used in the Shema to refer to God: "Hear, O Israel: The Lord [*kyrios*] our God is one Lord." He asserts that it was a short step from Elizabeth's proclamation of Mary as "mother of our

Lord" to Mary as *Theotokos* (mother of God), which in turn fueled the idea of the Immaculate Conception.[13]

The phrase "blessed among women" (also occurring in Luke 1:28) is viewed by Catholic theologians as alluding to the Eve-Mary comparison. Unlike Eve, who was cursed for her disobedience, Mary is blessed for her obedience.[14] Popular devotion to the idea of Mary as "blessed among women" was assured when Pope Urban II ordered the phrase to be used by both regular and secular clergy to secure Mary's help for the first Crusade in 1095.[15] The idea of Mary being blessed "among" women was viewed to mean that she was set apart from other women. As this interpretation was embraced, Mary, now viewed as blessed and sinless, became the ideal to whom women, and men, should strive to imitate.

The third scripture cited is Genesis 3:15 (*Protoevangelium*). The Douay-Rheims translation from the Vulgate reads, "I will put enmities between thee and the woman, and thy seed and her seed: she shall crush thy head, and thou shalt lie in wait for her heel." Most other translations render the second part of the passage as "He shall bruise thy head, and thou shalt bruise his heel." "The seed of the woman" is commonly understood to be messianic, that is Jesus Christ, the God-Man, the Redeemer. Thus "the woman" is understood to be the mother of the seed, Mary. As early as the second century[16] some held to this interpretation, that there is a direct link between Mary and Christ as victors over Satan. Irenaeus spoke of Mary in this way when he discussed the "doctrine of recapitulation of all things in Christ." He wrote, "If, then, the first-made man's sin was mended by the right conduct of the firstborn Son [of God], and if the serpent's cunning was bested by the simplicity of the dove [Mary], and if the chains that held us bound to death have been broken, then the heretics are fools …"[17]

Although Mary is seen here as having power over Satan, this was not typically taught as doctrine within the Catholic Church. However, later scholars and more contemporary Catholic theologians (Pope Pius XII in 1953,[18] Pope John Paul II in 1996[19]) used this interpretation to bolster the dogma of the Immaculate Conception. They argued that Mary's victory over Satan would not have been perfect if she had ever been under his dominion. Consequently, she must have entered this world without the stain of original sin.[20]

Once "the seed of the woman" is linked to Christ and Mary, it is a short step to seeing Mary as a second Eve. On one hand, Mary, the Immaculate Conception, is seen as a replica of Eve in purity and integrity before the Fall.²¹ On the other hand, she is viewed as the antithesis of Eve: where Eve disobeyed, Mary was obedient. Pelikan links this typology to Paul's reference to Jesus as the "second Adam" (Romans 5:19).²² While the first man, Adam introduced sin into the world, the second Adam, Jesus, brought redemption from sin. Marian scholars link the typology of the first man/second man to the first sinless woman, Eve, who disobeyed God, to the second sinless woman, Mary, who obeyed, even though this connection is never made in Scripture. Gambero points to the root of the idea of this connection being first established by Irenaeus:

> Eve was seduced by the word of the [fallen] angel and transgressed God's word, so that she fled from him. In the same way, [Mary] was evangelized by the word of an angel and obeyed God's word, so that she carried him [within her]. And while the former was seduced into obeying God, the latter was persuaded to obey God, so that the Virgin Mary became the advocate of the virgin Eve. And just as the human race was bound to death because of a virgin, so it was set free from death by a Virgin, since the disobedience of one virgin was counterbalanced by a Virgin's obedience.²³

Ott points out that while the Immaculate Conception was not explicitly taught by the early Greek or Latin Fathers, they did teach it implicitly through the teaching of two fundamental ideas: Mary's most perfect purity and holiness, and the similarity and contrast between Mary and Eve.²⁴ Neither idea originated in Scripture. This entire string of events provided the foundation for the establishment of the Immaculate Conception as doctrine. The vision seen by Catherine Laboure was the catalyst that led to the desire of the people and the ideas of Catholic theologians to coalesce into the formal statement of this doctrine.

Four years after the Immaculate Conception was established as dogma, another series of apparitions further increased the popularity of Marian devotion. Between February 11 and July 16, 1858, a poor, illiterate French girl, Bernadette Soubirous, had visions of "something white in the shape of a girl" in the grotto of Massabielle. According to the extensive written accounts of these events, at first, Bernadette's friends and family ridiculed her. She returned to the grotto on February 14 and fell into a trance, which frightened her companions. They ran for help, and she was taken to the mill. By the time she woke up, a crowd had gathered. Bernadette said she had seen a pretty, young girl with a rosary. Four days later, she was back at the grotto, this time with two women. The Aquero (Bernadette's name for the vision) spoke and asked her to return in two weeks. As it was market day, news of the vision spread throughout the countryside.

The number of people who came to the grotto increased daily. When Bernadette next arrived at the site, she was surprised to see between two hundred and three hundred people. She was astounded that they did not see the vision or hear her conversation. The ninth apparition occurred on February 25. This time, Bernadette was told to wash in the spring and drink some of the water. Seeing nothing but mud, she wiped the mud on her face and swallowed some of the muddy water. People were disgusted by her behavior, and many thought she was crazy. When questioned, Bernadette told them the apparition looked like one of the statues in her church, except she was alive and surrounded by light.

Despite being threatened by her family and civil authorities, Bernadette continued to return to the grotto. On March 2, more than fifteen hundred people gathered there. Soldiers were called in to control the crowds. That evening, when Bernadette was questioned by one of the Church officials, she said the Aquero had asked for a procession to be made to the grotto and for a chapel to be built there. By March 4, the end of the two-week period, three thousand to four thousand people were in attendance. They expected a miracle, but they were disappointed. Bernadette fell into a trance, as usual, but when she awoke, she told the Church official that she still did not know the apparition's name. At the time, the appearance of the spring was not considered a miraculous event as the source of the spring in the grotto was known by local shepherds.

Bernadette did not return until March 24, the Feast of the Annunciation. By now there were only fifty to a hundred people. This time, when Bernadette asked the apparition's name, she was told, "I am the Immaculate Conception." The last two times she saw the apparition were on

April 7, when the vision again asked for a chapel to be built, and on July 16, the feast of Our Lady of Mount Carmel. For a long time after the visions, Bernadette suffered illnesses.

The popularity of the site continued to grow, despite local opposition. The Catholic Church conducted an investigation and published its findings in January 1862—the Virgin had truly appeared to Bernadette—and the cult of Our Lady of Lourdes was established. In 1864 an image of the Virgin as described by Bernadette was blessed and installed at the site. Bernadette returned on May 21, 1866, and attended mass at the small chapel that had been built at the apparition's request. She entered a convent and reportedly spent the remainder of her life suffering both physically and spiritually.[25]

The Church of the Immaculate Conception was completed in 1872 and was celebrated with a torchlight procession. A medical bureau was established in 1884 to substantiate reported miracles that were being attributed to the spring of water that issued forth from the grotto. This shrine became the most visited center of Marian devotion in the world. The fame of Mary as healer grew with it. Bernadette's visions continue to draw people to venerate the Virgin.

Two other visions of Mary occurred during this time. In 1846, she was reportedly seen by two children, Melanie Calvat and Maximum Giraud. The children were warned about a coming famine and were each told a secret they were not to reveal. The Virgin was said to be very sad, because people did not honor her Sabbath and used her Son's name as a swearword. In 1851, although some of the local people had reservations, the site of the apparition at La Salette was approved by the bishop of Grenoble. A sanctuary was built on the site, and many miracles and conversions reportedly occurred there. The fate of the children mirrored Bernadette's. Melanie tried to live as a nun in several different convents and claimed to have other visions. She eventually wrote a book revealing her secret, but the Catholic Church intervened and stopped her from publishing it. Maximum tried to be a priest, failed, went into debt, and died of a heart attack after visiting the shrine at La Salette. He was forty years old.[26]

One other late nineteenth-century vision was recognized by the Church. On January 17, 1871, two children in Pontmain said they saw a vision of the Virgin dressed in a blue robe covered with stars and wearing a black veil. Their mother told neighbors that her boys were seeing the

Virgin surrounded by a frame and candles with a red cross on her breast. As the neighbors began to pray, the children said the apparition grew in size. Each time the people said another Marian prayer, messages appeared at her feet. In the evening, a white veil covered the apparition, and she reportedly vanished. Official acknowledgement of the vision was granted by the Church in 1872. The Basilica of Pontmain was complete in 1877.

The series of apparitions and the accounts of miracles that accompanied them greatly increased popular Marian devotion. The impact was so great, and their influence on dogma within the Catholic Church was so profound, that the era has been referred to as the Marian Age.[27] Congregations were dedicated specifically to the Virgin, e.g., Society of Missionaries of Mary (1853), Congregation of Mary Reparatrice (1854). In 1855 the Catholic Church approved the public veneration of the Heart of Mary.[28]

As devotion to Mary grew, and pilgrimages to sites of the visions at Lourdes and La Salette increased in number, opposition to the Catholic Church also grew. When the declaration of Papal Infallibility was proclaimed to be dogma 1870, people in Germany and France moved away from the Church. Things were not peaceful within the Church, either. When Leo XIII became pope in February of 1878, he and the Church faced many problems. He recommended that the faithful seek strength through the recitation of the Rosary and affirmed that grace comes only through Mary, "as no one can come to the highest Father except through the Son, so hardly anyone can come to the Son except through the Mother." He portrayed Mary as loving and Jesus as judge.[29]

In 1882, Matthias J. Scheeben published a work on Catholic dogma that showed the height to which Marian veneration had ascended. In the section on Mariology, Scheeben posited that the Eve-Mary comparison was not completely accurate since Eve was Adam's wife, whereas Mary was the mother of Jesus. He also rejected the idea that Mary would have any authority over Jesus as a human mother. Rather than moving away from this idea of Mary as a second Eve, Scheeben proposed that Mary's influence over her Son, as taught by the Church, is better represented by a bride's influence over her husband. Therefore, Mary should be considered in every sense the spiritual Bride of God whose spiritual Bridegroom is her Son.[30] Scheeben's theology is representative of the kind of thinking that was spawned by the growing interest in Mariology; thinking that mirrors ancient goddess theology.

While Scheeben's theology of Mary did not directly become Catholic teaching, it did leave its mark. He posited that veneration due Mary was neither worship, due only to God, nor the mere veneration due to all of the saints. Rather, he wrote, the veneration due Mary should be viewed as *hyperdulia*, a sort of super-veneration differing in kind and intensity from the veneration of saints.[31] This term became part of Catholic terminology.

The visions that had such an impact on the growth of Marian veneration and the declaration that the Immaculate Conception was dogma continued into the early twentieth century. Three twentieth-century visions were officially recognized. The first was in Fatima, a village in Portugal. On May 13, 1917, three children—the oldest was Lucia, age ten—saw flashes of light and then a lady standing above a tree. The apparition told them to return on the thirteenth of each month for the next six months and that she would reveal her name on the seventh visit. As with the other visions, each succeeding appearance drew greater crowds: from sixty in June to about seventy thousand in October. In 1922, a Church commission was formed to investigate the visions. Seven years later, although the apparition's pronouncements did not come to pass, the commission approved the visions. In 1930, Pope Pius XI granted indulgences for visits to the shrine. In 1942, in celebration of the twenty-fifth anniversary of the apparitions, Pope Pius XII proclaimed the consecration of the world to the Immaculate Heart of Mary. Ten years later, he proclaimed a special consecration of Russia in accordance with the demand the Blessed Virgin told to Lucia. The consecration of Russia was supposed to lead to Russia's conversion. That has still not happened.[32]

The other two recognized apparitions occurred in Belgium: Beauraing in 1932 and Banneux in 1933. Graef records that the Catholic Church investigated no fewer than thirty series of visions between 1930 and 1950. Whereas only three twentieth-century visions were given official recognition, the impact was nonetheless felt among the faithful.

The reason so many of the Catholic faithful were willing to believe in the validity of these visions lies in the tradition of the bodily Assumption of Mary. According to Perry's research, three early writings influenced this tradition. In the fourth century, Cyril of Jerusalem wrote that the apostles lost Mary's body as they fled a Jewish mob determined to mutilate it during her funeral procession. He says nothing about Mary's miraculous entry into heaven. In a so-called eyewitness account by Bishop Evodius of Rome (dates uncertain), Christ appeared to Mary and the apostles, received her soul at her death, and then reappeared seven months later to reunite Mary's soul and body and take both to heaven. The third text, allegedly by the apostle John but not found in Scripture, shortens the timespan from death to assumption to three days. The account attributed to John proved to be the most popular and became the template for the official Western account by Melito of Sardis. (As this account does not appear in Scripture, its authenticity is suspect.) By the eighth century, the Assumption of Mary was widely and popularly believed, even if it was not officially approved.[33]

That official approval was finally given by Pius XII on November 1, 1950. Pius XII issued an encyclical, the *Munificentissimus Deus*, which defined the dogma of the Bodily Assumption of Mary, stating in part:

> Mary, by an entirely unique privilege, completely overcame sin by her immaculate conception, and as a result she was not subject to the law of remaining in corruption of the grave, and she did not have to wait until the end of time for the redemption of her body ... testimonies, indications and signs of this common belief of the Church ... from remote times down through the course of the centuries ... is shown by the number of temples dedicated to it, the many artworks depicting it, the consecration of places to her patronage and, of course, to the Rosary, which proposes the assumption as one of the seven mysteries to be contemplated ... [the earliest sermons delivered on this feast day] spoke of this doctrine as something known and accepted by Christ's faithful.[34]

Perry observes that Pius XII's declaration of the dogma of the Assumption was the culmination of previous honors given to Mary: Predestination, Immaculate Conception, Perpetual Virginity, and Divine Motherhood.[35] It is important to note that the declaration did not state that Mary was immortal, only that her body did not see corruption. This declaration was issued *ex cathedra*, meaning that it falls under the cover of infallibility of the pope. The doctrine of infallibility states that this teaching holds the same authority as the words of Jesus Christ and that as a doctrine of faith and morals, it is to be followed by the whole Church.

In 1954, Pius XII proclaimed a Marian Year to celebrate the centennial of the definition of the Immaculate Conception. He deliberately linked it to the Assumption and strongly encouraged bishops to promote Marian devotion through sermons and pilgrimages, especially to Lourdes.[36] On October 11, 1954, the pope closed the Marian Year with yet another encyclical, *Ad caeli reginam*. This proclamation established the feast of Mary as Queen of Heaven, a title that had been unofficially used for her since Boniface IX at the end of the fourteenth century.[37] These proclamations were important steps in solidifying the doctrine of Mary among the Magisterium of the Catholic Church. They also added to the scope of Marian veneration that already was solidly entrenched in the faith and practice of the laity.

Chapter 18

The veneration of Mary had again become fully entrenched in the hearts and actions of the laity, just as it was before the Enlightenment. Yet, this devotion, in practice, did not mirror the official position of the Magisterium of the Church. The Catholic Church declared explicitly that devotion due to Mary is not the same as worship due to the Trinity. This devotion "is not *latria* [Greek: *latreia*, worship], for *worship* or *adoration* belongs to God alone; nor is it mere *dulia* [Greek: *doulia*, service], for *veneration* is given to all saints; but it is *hyperdulia*, or *super-veneration*, which is reserved for her."[1] Hyperdulia, in practice, seems very much like goddess and emperor worship of ancient times. Marian feast days, both local and universal, are common in Catholic communities around the world. One count of Marian feast days listed 465, of which only forty-seven were celebrated by the entire Catholic Church. These often included processions with an image of the Virgin, as called for by the apparition in some of the visions. In predominantly Catholic countries, it is not unusual to see statues of Mary decorated with flowers on country roads and at intersections. They bear a striking resemblance to temple goddesses that in ancient times were found in virtually every major city.

In a similar way, since the fourth century, countless churches and shrines have been built to honor Mary under her various names. Some of these are well known and receive millions of visitors each year. During the two-day celebration of the 478th anniversary of the apparition of the Virgin of Guadalupe, 6.1 million people were in attendance. This is not an unusual occurrence: the chapel of Our Lady of Guadalupe in Mexico[2] can hold 50,000 people at once. Veneration of Our Lady of Lourdes in France is just as popular; up to five million people visit the shrine annually.[3]

Other shrines are smaller and draw more local attention. At the shrine dedicated to Our Lady of San Juan del Valle in San Juan, Texas, one can see hundreds of letters written to the Virgin in thanksgiving for healing and other answered prayers attributed directly to her. Many of these are accompanied by discarded crutches, flowers, candles, and other offerings.[4] Shrines often are erected to commemorate the report of a miraculous event, such as the visions of Bernadette at Lourdes. Then people visit the site to offer their prayers to the mother of God. As its popularity increases, the site is eventually consecrated by a local bishop. Catholic churches named for Christ or saints nearly always have chapels where the faithful can offer their devotion to the Mary in prayer, gifts, and lighting of candles. Millions of young girls have been named for Mary. Hundreds of thousands of men as well as women have followed her "example of the virginal life," dedicating their lives to the service of God in her honor in the vocations of priest or nun. The desire of the laity to continue in adoration of Mary that had been reinforced by the utterings of the apparitions concerned some of the more conservative members of the Magisterium.

In response to this concern, Pope John XXIII called for the Second Vatican Council (Vatican II) to be held beginning in 1962. Regarding the discussion of the breadth and scope of Marian veneration, there were two schools of thought. Marian maximalists were pleased to see the number of declarations and feasts to Mary increasing. They looked forward to the council giving Mary the title Mediatrix of all Graces. There were those who also hoped to see the declaration of the definition of Mary as co-redemptrix, making her effectively equal to her Son in the process of salvation. Marian minimalists opposed these ideas. They were influenced by movements both inside and outside the Catholic Church toward ecumenism and, thus, sought a return to more scriptural teaching. They believed Marian devotion had grown out of proportion and wanted to see a purification of the veneration of the Virgin. Part of their argument centered on whether Mary should be included in the overall discussion regarding the nature of the Church or considered separately. John XXIII, a minimalist who sought church unity, died on June 3, 1963. The College of Cardinals elected maximalist Paul VI who dedicated his office to the Virgin Mary. When the 2,188 participants voted, 313 of them voted in favor of Mary being included, specifically in the context of her mediation (i.e., the maximalist position).

On November 21, 1964, Pope Paul VI (1963–78) issued the *Lumen gentium*, a dogmatic statement on the nature of the Church. It was approved by 2,151 of the 2,156 bishops assembled and clearly takes the minimalist position about the Virgin Mary. Although the statement references medieval and modern texts, the Council sought to ground Mariology in the earliest (common) Christian faith. The text asserts that Mary is the beloved daughter of the Father, temple of the Holy Spirit, and was predestined to be the mother of the Son of God. There are privileges attached to her motherhood and her free assent to it. Yet, these privileges do not make her divine. She is still one of the offspring of Adam and one with all those who are to be saved. At the same time, the statement asserts that she is an exalted creature, highest after Christ and closest to mankind. As such, she is to be hailed as preeminent and a wholly unique member of the church; she is its exemplar and outstanding model in faith and charity. The Church honors her with the filial affection and devotion rightly due to the most beloved Mother of the Church.[5]

This document did not change official declarations of the past or negate some unofficial statements that had become Marian tradition. It did, however, diminish the sense of Mary as part of the godhead. Instead, it established her as a representative of the human race (as a daughter of Adam and as the new Eve) and a representative of all believers (as a picture of the church and as a model for Christian life).[6] Furthermore, the document specified that Mary's roles as mediator and co-redemptrix do not make her equal to Christ. Rather even in these, she is a role model for all believers. "She is unique only in the fullness of her response to and participation in it."[7] Against the advice of the majority of the bishops, Pope Paul VI declared a new Marian title: mother of the church. The minimalists objected to this title because it did not have a biblical basis, but the pope's authority stood.

Pope Paul VI also reopened dialogue regarding Marian apparitions. On December 29, 1970, he abolished Canon 1399, paragraph 5, of the Code of Canon Law, which forbade books and publications that described new apparitions, revelations, prophecies, miracles, and the launching of new devotions. The old Canon 2318, which allowed for the excommunication of those who offended against Canon 1399, was also suppressed.[8] While this pope's later actions supported Vatican II, this act left open the door for a future revival of Marian devotion connected to new apparitions.

On February 2, 1974, ten years after Vatican II issued the *Lumen Gentium*, Paul VI issued the *Marialis Cultus*—a call to implement reforms called for by Vatican II. These reforms, which centered on emphasizing Christ rather than Mary, initially resulted in an increase in ecumenism. As dialogue between Protestants and Catholics grew, so did Christ-centered movements within the Catholic Church. Movements such as the Charismatic Renewal and Cursillo (three days in Christian community aimed at spiritual renewal) produced a new breed of "born again" Catholics. This obvious devotion to Christ by many in the Catholic Church led evangelicals and Catholics alike to wonder if the gaps between them were not impassable after all.[9] Whereas many still seek common ground, the reemergence of Marian devotion has begun to diminish this hope.

One of the first acts of Pope John Paul II was to revive the cult of Mary. He made pilgrimages to all of the important Marian shrines and took for his motto *Totus Tuus sum Maria* (Mary, I am all yours). John Paul II gave Mary credit for saving his life during two assassination attempts in 1981 and 1982 and credited her with the fall of Communism in Eastern Europe. His popularity with the Catholic laity rekindled the passion for Marian devotion among large numbers of Catholics, particularly after apparitions of Mary appeared in Medjugorje, Yugoslavia.[10] The focus of *Don't Forget Mary*, a book by Pope Benedict XVI (2005–13), was a call for renewed Marian devotion.[11] He modeled this devotion by making his own pilgrimages to Marian shrines. When Francis (2013–present) was elected pope, his first encyclical closed with a prayer to Mary:

> Mother, help our faith! Open our ears to hear God's word and to recognize his voice and call. Awaken in us a desire to follow in his footsteps, to go forth from our own land and to receive his promise. Help us to be touched by his love, that we may touch him in faith. Help us to entrust ourselves fully to him and to believe in his love, especially at times of trial, beneath the shadow of the cross, when our faith is called to mature. Sow in our faith the joy of the Risen One. Remind us that those who believe are never alone. Teach us to see all things with the eyes of Jesus, that he may be light for our path. And may this light of faith

> always increase in us, until the dawn of that undying day which is Christ himself, your Son, our Lord!¹²

It is clear from his prayer that Marian devotion has not been forgotten; the Catholic faithful are reminded to not forget their mother, Mother of the Church, and Queen of Heaven.

On the twentieth anniversary of the close of Vatican II, John Paul II called for a book to be published that would provide clarity on the doctrine and dogmas of the Catholic Church. *Catechism of the Catholic Church*, written by then Cardinal Joseph Ratzinger (later Benedict XVI) in 1994, specifies that while Mary resides bodily in heaven in an exalted position and is worthy of veneration, her function as mother of men does not obscure or diminish the unique mediation of Christ. The description of Mary as "the image and beginning of the church as it is to be perfected in the world" is further qualified: as a conduit for all grace and merit of Christ to men, she draws her power from Christ. There is a limit to Marian devotion, even though the Catholic Church holds a much higher view of her than is given by Scripture.¹³

While *Catechism* makes clear that prayer, led by the Holy Spirit, should always be to God, invoking the name of Jesus, prayer also is seen as uniting the faithful with Mary, His mother. The book lays out the biblical principal but reinforces the common practice, stating that Mary shows the way to her Son. According to this teaching, such filial prayer unites the faithful with the mother of Jesus. "Thus in countless hymns and antiphons expressing this prayer, two movements usually alternate with one another: the first magnifies the Lord for the 'great things' he did for his lowly servant and through *her* for all human beings; the second entrusts the supplications and praises of the children of God to the Mother of Jesus."¹⁴

Part III

A Biblical Response to Marian Tradition and Practice

Part III

Chapter 19

To provide a framework for a biblical response to Marian veneration, we must understand four foundational principles of Catholic faith and practice and their relationship to Mary's perceived place in the Church and its Economy of Salvation. The material in this section is taken primarily from *Catechism of the Catholic Church* by Joseph Cardinal Ratzinger, who was elected Pope Benedict XVI in 2005.

First, the authority of the Catholic Church is binding on people of faith, because it is believed to have a direct link to the authority of Christ. Principles defined as dogma hold places of particular importance and require Church members to adhere to these beliefs as direct teachings of Christ, even if they have no solid basis in Scripture. According to *Catechism*, the Magisterium of the Catholic Church (the pope and bishops) derives its authority directly from Christ. It exercises this authority to the fullest extent when it proposes truths contained in, or connected to, divine revelation. These propositions are then defined in a form that obliges Catholics to respond with an irrevocable adherence of faith. Thus, when the Immaculate Conception was declared dogma, the pope's declaration was considered to be equal in weight to the word of Christ.[1]

Second, the source of faith and practice in the Catholic Church is not solely Scripture, that is, the sixty-six books of the authorized Bible. The Catholic Church recognizes three things as having equal weight: Tradition (which has been our focus here); sacred scripture (which includes the seventy-three books of the Apocrypha); and the teaching of the Magisterium. All three are credited to being empowered by the Holy Spirit to work together for the salvation of souls.[2]

Catechism teaches that scripture (seventy-three books) should be read in light of Church tradition. Thus, when one reads scripture concerning Mary, it should be done so with full belief in the tradition of the Church that developed through the centuries.³ This is in stark contrast to the teaching of evangelicals, who hold that Scripture alone (sixty-six books) is all that holds authority for faith and practice in Christian life.

Scripture and Tradition are equaled in authority by the Magisterium, which is made up of the pope and the bishops. The teaching of the Magisterium is believed to be infallible: what the pope and bishops decree is considered to have the same weight as the words of Jesus recorded in scripture. This infallibility extends to all elements of doctrine.⁴ Therefore, the teaching of the Catholic Church regarding Mary's place in the Economy of Salvation is binding on all members of that body.⁵ This was verified in the papal bull issued by Pius XII that established the doctrine of the Assumption of Mary: "all those things are to be believed by divine and Catholic faith which are contained in the written Word of God or in Tradition, and which are proposed by the Church, either in solemn judgment or in its ordinary and universal teaching office, as divinely revealed truths which must be believed."⁶

Third, when referring to scripture, the Catholic Bible includes books that are not recognized by Protestants and evangelicals as part of the received canon. The writings the Catholic Church considers sacred scripture were included based on their use in Church tradition. Catholic scripture includes forty-six books in the Old Testament and twenty-seven in the New Testament.⁷ Six of the Old Testament books were not part of the Hebrew Bible and also were rejected as not inspired during the Protestant Reformation. This is important because much of the teaching about Mary is grounded in these extra books as well as in Tradition and teaching of the Magisterium.

Fourth, the process of salvation extends beyond an acknowledgment of faith in Jesus Christ as Savior. The Catholic Church recognizes seven sacraments. These are taught to be powers that come forth from the Body of Christ (the Catholic Church). *Catechism* explains that the Holy Spirit works through these sacraments, rendering them as conduits for spiritual and eternal life.⁸ The first three sacraments—baptism, confirmation, and the Eucharist—are considered the foundations that initiate Christian life. Penance and the anointing of the sick (Extreme Unction) are sacraments of healing. The last two, holy orders and matrimony, are recognized as sacraments in which only some believers participate. The Catholic Church teaches that these sacraments are *necessary for salvation*.[9] According to this teaching, the grace of the Holy Spirit is associated with, and flows through, the sacraments. This grace, given by Christ, heals and transforms those who receive the Spirit through the Sacraments by conforming them to the Son of God. Those who participate in the sacramental life—minimally baptism, confirmation and the Eucharist—reap the fruit of the Spirit contained therein: the spirit of adoption that unites them in a living union with the only Son of God.

The Catholic Church teaches that it is through baptism that one is given spiritual birth and enters the Church, the Body of Christ.[10] Confirmation perfects the grace given at baptism and is the sacrament through which the Holy Spirit is given.[11] The Eucharist is the source and highest point of ecclesial life. The other sacraments are bound up with the Eucharist and are oriented toward it. In Catholic tradition and teaching, the bread and wine of the Eucharist contain the whole spiritual good of the Church, namely Christ himself.[12] The doctrine of transubstantiation teaches that the bread and wine offered in the Eucharist are truly the body and blood of Christ. Thus by ingesting them, the believer becomes united with Christ and the Church.

For our purposes, it is not necessary to discuss the anointing of the sick, holy orders, or matrimony. However, it is in the understanding of penance and its role in the economy of salvation of the Catholic Church that we will see the part Mary plays.

Mary's Place in the Church

According to Catholic teaching, Mary has two roles in the life of the believer. First, as Mother of the Church, she can be petitioned in prayer to intercede on behalf of the believer to her Son, Jesus Christ, for mercy. The faithful may call on her for protection from danger and to meet their needs. Devotion to Mary, expressed through feasts and prayers, such as the Rosary, are proper and encouraged. She is seen as the mother of the church because she is the mother of Christ.

According to *Catechism*, Mary's maternal role in the work of salvation flows out of her inseparable union with her Son from the time of His virginal conception until His death, and most particularly during His Passion. After Christ ascended to heaven, tradition holds that Mary helped establish the early church through her prayers. After her death, the Immaculate Virgin—who, according to tradition, was preserved from the stain of original sin and who lived a sinless life—was taken to heaven, body and soul. There she is said to be exalted as queen of all things, thereby conforming her more fully to the Lord of Lords and the conqueror of sin and death. From this position as mother of God, the new Eve, and the mother of the church, Mary exercises her maternal role on behalf of followers of Christ. The Virgin Mary is to serve as a model of faith and charity through her example of obedience, faith, hope, and burning charity in the Savior's work of restoring supernatural life to souls. Mary is seen as the mother of the faithful in the order of grace. Because of her position, she is to be invoked by the church through the titles of Advocate, Helper, Benefactress, and Mediatrix and is to be recognized as the conduit of all grace.[13]

Mary's Place in the Economy of Salvation

Mary's second role is seen in the Economy of Salvation, particularly in regard to the sacrament of penance. According to the teaching of the Catholic Church, the result of sin is two-fold: it results in a loss of communion with God, and it is damaging to the believer and therefore to the Body of Christ.

Penance, in its various parts, has three purposes: to restore the first consequence of sin; to restore communion with God; and to heal the damage caused by sin. The sacrament of penance is described as a three-part process. Two parts are actions of the penitent. The third is an action of the priest. The penitent's two acts are repentance and confession. The goal of these two steps is to make reparation for sin and to do works that are evidence of this repentance.

If penitents truly desire to obtain reconciliation with God and the Church, they must confess all unconfessed "grave" sins they remember to the priest. Note that the Catholic Church teaches that a person can commit two levels of sin: mortal (grave) and venial sin. Confession is the first of the penitent's two actions. The priest then will propose certain acts that the penitent should perform to repair the harm that sin caused to his or her relationship with God and the Church. According to this teaching, completion of the actions of penance directed by the priest has six spiritual effects:

1. The penitent is reconciled to God and recovers the grace lost.
2. The penitent is reconciled to the Church.
3. There is remission of the eternal punishment that was due to the commission of the mortal sin.
4. There is at least partial remission of the temporal punishment due to commission of the sin. (Note that the Catholic Church teaches two consequences of sin: eternal and temporal.)
5. The conscience of the penitent is restored to peace and serenity, and he or she receives spiritual consolation.
6. The penitent is given spiritual strength for his or her Christian life

Confession of grave sins followed by absolution remains the only ordinary means of reconciliation with God and with the Church. However, through indulgences, the faithful can obtain the remission of the temporal punishment that results from sin—for themselves and also for the souls in purgatory, which is where the deceased undergo purification so they can achieve the holiness required for entry into heaven.[14]

Three main points are important for our purposes. First, the Catholic Church recognizes levels of sin. Second, these sins require varying levels of eternal or temporal punishment to restore the sinner's relationship with God and the Church. Third, if absolution is not obtained in this life through the sacrament of penance, then after death, the soul of the believer will have to complete its punishment in purgatory in order to be purified of the consequences of sin.

The means of purification in purgatory is the treasury of merit (prayers and good works). According to Catholic teaching, the treasury of merit consists of all of the merits of Christ's work. It also contains the merit of Mary and the saints that exceeded what they needed to enter into heaven based on a works-based theology. This teaching holds that while one drop of Christ's blood was sufficient to save the world from the eternal effects of original sin (eternal separation from God, or hell), the rest of the blood He shed was deposited into a treasury that could be drawn on to compensate for the penalty of sin committed in one's lifetime (temporal sin). It is this sin that must be compensated for through merit.

The Catholic Church teaches that the work of the individual is never sufficient to compensate for the punishment due for temporal sin. However the Christian who seeks to purify himself of his sin does not have to accomplish this compensation alone. In this view of salvation, the life of each of God's children is joined in Christ to the life of all other Christian brethren in the supernatural unity of the Mystical Body of Christ. For this reason, a perineal link of charity is said to exist between the faithful who have already reached their heavenly home, those who are atoning for their sins in purgatory, and those who are still pilgrims on earth. Because they are all one body, there is said to be an abundant exchange of all good things. Thus the holiness, or merit, of one profits the others. This is the Church's Treasury of Merit. It is believed to be inexhaustible. The Catholic Church acknowledges that the satisfactions and merits of Christ's redemption are at work. However, Christ's work alone is apparently not sufficient, as the treasury also includes the prayers and good works of the Virgin Mary, which are said to be truly immense, unfathomable, and even pristine in their value before God. The treasury also includes the prayers and good works of all those the Catholic Church has proclaimed as saints.[15]

The Catholic Church holds that certain of an individual's own actions can work toward paying off the debt due for temporal sin. Attending certain Church functions, such as youth conferences, may be proclaimed by the pope to fall into this category. Wearing of scapulars or medals, with the related adherence to the role of the sponsoring confraternity, are particularly beneficial. The treasury may be drawn on for the balance due through the use of indulgences,[16] which can be secured from the Church by individuals for themselves or on behalf of those who have died. The goal of each of these actions is to shorten the individual's time in purgatory.

It is in the concepts of temporal sin, purgatory, and the treasury of merit that the role of Mary as a contributor to the Economy of Salvation is clearly defined. The Catholic Church, as we have seen, teaches that Mary was sinless and that she suffered, along with her Son, when He was crucified.[17] Therefore, in her roles as Mother of God, Queen of Heaven, representative of the Bride of Christ and Mother of the Church, her intercession is believed to have infinite value. Because Mary is viewed as the dispenser of all grace, one may recover lost grace by asking Mary to intercede. One may, and should, ask for Mary to intercede with her Son in seeking reconciliation with God the Father and with the Church.[18] One may petition Mary in prayer for her intercession in the process of remission of punishment for temporal sin. One may ask Mary to distribute the peace and serenity of conscience and spiritual consolation that is available from the Holy Spirit. One may even petition her for strength in the Christian battle against sin and temptation.[19] Because the Trinity as seen as the head of the church, Mary is viewed as the neck: all that God has for man is viewed as coming through Mary.[20]

Clearly the teachings of the Magisterium regarding Mary's place in the Church and in the Economy of Salvation continue to fuel Marian veneration among the laity. Vatican II sought to put Marian veneration into proper perspective, calling for the focus of worship to be on God the Father and His Son, our Savior, Jesus Christ. However, the failure to change the major doctrines and dogmas of Mary that were the root of veneration excesses weakened the effort and left the door open for excesses to recur. Evidence for the existence of this root could be seen at a recent Catholic conference attended by the author.

In April 2012, the Orange County Catholic Charismatic Renewal group held a conference at the Anaheim Convention Center. This three-day conference, attended by thousands of people from all over the United States, celebrated the forty-fifth anniversary of the beginning of the Catholic charismatic movement and was a vivid example of the success and failure of Vatican II. The first day began with worship. For nearly an hour, attendees, led by a praise team, sang praise songs that glorified Christ. The praise songs, the same ones used in evangelical worship, were sung with joy and enthusiasm; clearly, they were familiar to the attendees. However, once that worship time ended, a moderator got up and proclaimed, "Let us remember our Mother, Mary." A picture of Mary was set on the dais to the right of the crucifix (where it remained for the remainder of the conference), and the faithful recited the Hail Mary. This was followed by a prayer to Mary for the protection of students attending the youth conference in the adjacent hotel. The main speakers at the conference were all exorcists who had been trained in Rome. In each case, they proclaimed that the power for healing resided in the name of Jesus Christ alone. At the end of each session, prayer for protection over the following session was offered to Mary. As is typical with conventions, there was a large hall filled with vendors. While nearly every vendor had some Marian items, about half of them focused primarily on statues of Mary, rosaries, and Marian-themed devotionals, jewelry, and candles.[21]

This conference represented the effect Vatican II had on the veneration of Mary. Though the liturgy is more Christ focused, the hearts of the people still gravitate toward veneration of His mother. Should a series of apparitions similar to those of the late nineteenth and early twentieth centuries occur during a period of global turmoil today, it is easy to see how these roots might again blossom into the religious fervor for Mary that existed before Vatican II. A soundly biblical viewpoint of Mary is needed to keep the interpretation of her true position in proper perspective.

Chapter 20

There are two levels of Catholic belief: doctrine and dogma. Doctrine refers to all Church teaching in matters of faith and morals. These teachings are considered to have been divinely revealed to the leaders of the Church. Dogma is more narrowly defined. When an idea or point of doctrine is formally spelled out and is declared by the Magisterium to have been revealed as a matter to be believed by the Church members, it becomes dogma. The Catholic faithful are obliged to adhere to dogma and to follow whatever manner of action the Church requires to bear witness to that faith. Protestants and evangelicals do not have this distinction and cite only doctrine.

The Catholic Church holds to four dogmas concerning the Virgin Mary: Divine Motherhood, the Immaculate Conception, Perpetual Virginity, and the Assumption. As the Virgin Birth, here listed as Divine Motherhood, is a foundational point of faith in all of Christianity and fully established in Scripture, we will consider only the remaining three, which do not appear to be taught in the Bible's sixty-six books.

Immaculate Conception

The Immaculate Conception of Mary, as we have seen, was declared dogma by Pope Pius IX in 1854. The belief that Mary lived a sinless life flows logically from this premise. There are three primary reasons that evangelicals reject the dogma of the Immaculate Conception and implied sinless nature of Mary. The first is the doctrine of *sola scriptura* (or scripture alone), which holds that the sixty-six books of the Bible are the supreme and sole authority for all matters of faith and practice. As such, the Bible is the sole and direct revelation of God. It alone has divine authority. The Bible is the sufficient, final, and infallible the Word of God—all that is necessary to ignite faith and guide life. This does not mean that everything in the Bible is perfectly clear, but rather that all essential biblical teachings are clear. In the matter of interpretation, one is to look to Scripture alone.[1] This contradicts the Catholic idea that tradition and the teaching of the Magisterium have equal weight; among evangelicals, the Bible, alone, is authoritative.

The second reason is also related to the canon of scripture: whereas the Catholic Church includes the apocryphal books as valid for teaching, evangelicals hold that only the sixty-six books of the Bible recognized by the council of Laodicea (363-64) are necessary for Christian faith and practice. Evangelicals reject as non-canonical the apocryphal books because they were not added by the Catholic Church until the Council of Trent (1546). Most of the doctrine and dogma of the Catholic Church concerning Mary are included in these extra books.

The third reason evangelicals reject the Immaculate Conception is church history: evangelicals point out that from the very beginning of the church, there has been opposition to placing Mary in a higher position than other Christians. This begins in scripture with Jesus himself. In the Gospel of Luke, we read an account of Jesus being confronted by a woman who proclaims, "Blessed is the womb that bore you and the breasts at which you nursed!" Jesus does not condone this elevation of His mother. He responds, "On the contrary, blessed are those who hear the Word of God and observe it" (Luke 11:27–28). The Gospel of Matthew states that Jesus placed His mother with other believers.

> While He was still speaking to the crowds, behold His mother and brothers were standing outside seeking to speak to Him. Someone said to Him, "Behold, your mother and your brothers are standing outside seeking to speak to you." But Jesus answered the one who was telling Him and said, "Who is my mother and who are my brothers?" And stretching out His hand toward His disciples, He said, "Behold my mother and my brothers! For whoever does the will of my Father who is in heaven, he is my brother and sister and mother" (Matthew 12:46–50).

Why Mary?

Later in Scripture, we see that Mary has joined the disciples of Jesus. She is with them in the upper room when the gift of the Holy Spirit is poured out on them all. Yet, at this point in the ministerial life of Jesus, she is apparently still on the outside. In fact, the Gospel of Mark records that Jesus's mother and brothers did not have a very high view of His teaching early on. Mark tells us that Jesus had been out in the countryside, preaching,

> And He came home [to Capernaum], and the crowd gathered again to such an extent that they could not even eat a meal. When His own people [His family] heard of this, they went out to take custody of Him; for they were saying, "He has lost His mind" (Mark 3:20–21).

As stated earlier, in the view of *sola scriptura*, correct translation and exegesis of scripture from the original language are the keys to arguing against the sinlessness of Mary. The three passages of Scripture that have been presented as foundations for Catholic doctrine and dogma regarding the Immaculate Conception of Mary are Luke 1:28, Luke 1:42–43, and Genesis 3:15. We will look at each to see why they do *not* provide the foundation for this dogma.

In Luke 1:28, the Catholic Church uses the Vulgate translation for the original Greek word κεχαριτωμένη, from the Greek verb χαριτόω, rendering it as "full of grace." Yet, most all other translations from the Greek render this passive participle as "highly favored." Manelli, a Catholic, points out that the Greek is not easily translatable: it may mean "highest in grace," "most beloved," "privileged," or "gratified." He believes this fullness of grace primarily means a spiritual state without excluding all that is physical. When taken in conjunction with the angel's greeting, *chaire*—which Manelli recognizes etymologically as "rejoice" but corresponding to the Latin *ave* meaning "hail"—he sees a special greeting that can be used only for Mary: "Rejoice, O Full of Grace."[2] However, evangelical scholars point out that the same verb for God's grace or favor on Mary, χαριτόω, is used to describe the grace God bestows on all people who are understood to be inherently sinful (Romans 3:23), but who believe in Christ as Savior and follow Him: "… His [God's] grace, which He freely bestowed on us in the Beloved [Jesus]." While the connection between the two words is difficult to see in translation, it is very clear in the original Greek. In *The IVP New Testament Commentary* on Luke 1:28–46, Darrell Bock clearly presents a biblical view of Mary:

> She is a model believer, taking God at His word ... She is favored of God (v. 30), thoughtful (vv. 37–38), obedient (v. 38), believing (v. 45), worshipful (v. 46) and a faithful follower of God's law (2:22–51). It must be emphasized, however, that despite all of these qualities, God's choice of Mary to bear His Child springs from His grace, not from any inherent merit she possesses. She is the object of God's unmerited, graciously provided goodness. Her description as one who has found *favor with God* (*kecharitomene*, v. 30) makes it clear that God has acted on her behalf and not because of her. In fact, Mary is totally perplexed by the sudden announcement. She did not ask for this role in God's plans; God has simply stepped into her life and brought her into His service. Her asset is that she is faithful. She should be honored for her faithfulness and openness to serve God, but that does not mean she is to be worshipped. Luke wants us to identify with Mary's example, not to unduly exalt her position.[3]

According to Catholic thought, because it would be reasonable to assume that a perfect vessel would be preferable for the gestation of God in a human womb, it would follow that Mary would have been given God's grace in forgiveness of her sins before the Holy Spirit came upon her, initiating the growth of the infant Jesus in her womb. The Magisterium further reasons that, because God could have given his grace to Mary before she was born, it is reasonable to assume He did so. Hence, there is the Immaculate Conception, which refers to Mary as being born without sin. Tied to this thinking is the idea that God predestined Mary for this purpose. In his *Catechism*, Ratzinger writes "... from all eternity God chose for the mother of his Son a daughter of Israel, a young Jewish woman of Nazareth in Galilee, a Virgin betrothed to a man whose name was Joseph, of the house of David; and the virgin's name was Mary."[4]

The idea of predestination to a specific task is certainly biblical. Scripture tells us that God predestines individuals for salvation, based on His foreknowledge of the choices they will make, using language that mirrors the "fullness of grace" the Catholic Church allots to Mary, alone of all people.

> Just as He [God] chose us in Him [Christ] before the foundation of the world, that we would be holy and blameless before Him [God]. In love He [God] predestined us to adoption as sons through Jesus Christ to Himself, according to the kind intention of His will, to the praise of the glory of His grace, which He freely bestowed on us in the Beloved [Christ]. In Him [Christ] we have redemption through His blood, the forgiveness of our trespasses, according to the riches of His [God's] grace which He lavished on us (Ephesians 1:4–8).

Just as God chose Mary to bear the Son of God, He chooses others to bear His Son to the world through their testimony. Scripture tells us that John the Baptist, who was chosen to proclaim the coming of Christ and who baptized Jesus at the beginning of His ministry, was similarly chosen by God. An angel told John's father Zacharias that "he [John] will be great in the sight of the Lord ... and he will be filled with the Holy Spirit while yet in his mother's womb" (Luke 1:15). The apostle Paul also attests to this idea of God's grace being poured out on those He has chosen for His work. Paul writes concerning his own calling, "But when God, who had set me apart even from my mother's womb, and called me through His grace, was pleased to reveal His Son in me so that I might preach Him among the Gentiles ..." (Galatians 1:15–16). Paul also writes about the calling of God to all believers, "For we are His workmanship, created in Christ Jesus for good works, which God prepared beforehand that we should walk in them" (Ephesians 2:10). When we look at these, and other accounts of similar examples in scripture, we see that there is nothing remarkable about the idea of God choosing people for His work and pouring His grace upon them.

The dogma of Immaculate Conception—that is, the teaching that Mary was sinless from before her birth and continuously throughout her life—does not fit this scriptural pattern. In her article, "Mary, Servant of the Lord," Nancy Duff explains this problem succinctly:

> This emphasis on perfection contradicts the doctrine of incarnation summarized in Gabriel's proclamation that "the Lord is with you." That Mary was full of grace does not mean that she was created without sin in order to be *worthy* of giving birth to the Son of God, for God enters a world that is *unworthy* of the presence of God, a world that is sinful and broken. If Mary must be perfect in order to be worthy of carrying the Savior, the message is lost ... Mary's perfection ... presents a field of holiness capable of receiving God rather than the sinful and unworthy world in which God chooses to be present.[5]

The idea of the sinless perfection of Mary also contradicts Paul's teaching on the universality of sin. In his book *Christian Theology*, Millard Erickson discusses at length the Old Testament evidence of the foundational biblical teaching that all human beings, without exception, are born sinful. He goes on to address this principal in the writing of the apostle Paul.

> The New Testament is even clearer concerning the universality of human sin. The best known passage is ... Romans 3, where Paul quotes and elaborates upon Psalms 14 and 53, as well as 5:9, 140:3; 10:7; 36:1; and Isaiah 59:7–8. He asserts that "Jews and Gentiles alike are all under sin" (v. 9), and then heaps up a number of descriptive quotations beginning with, "There is no one righteous, not even one; there is no one who understands, no one who seeks God. All have turned away, they have together become worthless; there is no one who does good, *not even one*" (vv. 10–12, emphasis mine). None will be justified by works of the law (v. 20). The reason is clear: "for all have sinned and fall short of the glory of God" (v. 23). Paul also makes it plain that he is talking not only about unbelievers, those outside the Christian faith, but believers as well,

including himself. In Ephesians 2:3, he acknowledges that "all of us also lived among them [the sons of disobedience, v. 2] at one time gratifying the cravings of our sinful nature and following its desires and thoughts. Like the rest, we were by nature objects of wrath." It is apparent that there were no exceptions to this universal rule. In his statement on the law and its function, Paul makes mention of the fact that "Scripture declares that the whole world is a prisoner of sin" (Gal. 3:22). Similarly 1 John 5:19 indicates that "the whole world is under the control of the evil one."⁶

At no point does Scripture indicate that there are any exceptions to this universal shortcoming. Smith concurs: "The universality of sin is taken as a matter of fact. On examination, it will be found that every speech in Acts... and every Epistle just assumes that men have all sinned. This is also the assumption of Jesus in the Synoptic Gospels."⁷

Romans 6:23 makes clear that the universality of death is the result of the universality of sin. The Catholic Church's dogma regarding the bodily assumption of Mary does not state that Mary did not die, only that she ascended bodily to heaven. The teaching of Pius XII holds that Mary's sinlessness kept her body from corruption.⁸ However, Scripture is clear that sin and death are directly related; no reference is made to corruption of the body in the grave. If, as Catholicism teaches, Mary was born without sin because it was reasonable for God to create her sinless, would it not follow that it was reasonable for God to take her bodily to heaven without her having to suffer death?

Scripture recounts that two people were taken bodily to heaven without suffering death. Enoch "walked with God and was not, for God took him" (Genesis 5:24). Elisha witnessed Elijah being taken to heaven in a miraculous way. "As they were going along and talking, behold, there appeared a chariot of fire and horses of fire which separated the two of them. And Elijah went up by a whirlwind to heaven" (2 Kings 2:11). Scripture does not tell us that Enoch or Elijah were without sin. The pronouncement, that "all have sinned," apparently applies to them as well. Yet, they did not die.

If one follows the previously stated reasoning—that it was nobler for God to preserve Mary from sin than to redeem her from it—then similar logic would say that it would be nobler to take her to heaven without experiencing death rather than to have her die and then take her body to heaven. Nevertheless, the latter is not part of the dogma of the Assumption of Mary. Consequently, based on the clear statement of scripture, "the wages of sin is death" (Romans 6:23), and the fact that Mary did die, we can know that she was not sinless.

That Mary was subject to the judgment of God, and therefore not sinless, was posited by Hilary of Poitiers (300–368) in his *Tractus* on Psalm 118. In his discussion of the judgment of God in verse 12, he introduces the prophecy Simeon gave when Joseph and Mary presented the infant Jesus in the temple: "Behold this [Child] is appointed for the fall and rise of many in Israel and for a sign to be opposed—and a sword will pierce even your own soul ..." (Luke 2:34–35). Hilary saw this as a reference to Mary's recognition of her own susceptibility to judgment: "If even this Virgin who was capable of bearing God (*capax dei*) will come to the severity of judgment, who will dare to wish to be judged by God?"[9]

Other theologians also recognized that Mary was in need of purification and sanctification because of her human nature. Augustine (354–430) wrote in *Letter 164* that Christ Jesus did, indeed, take from the Virgin the true substance of the flesh, but that it was not "sinful flesh." This was not because Mary was sinless, but because the flesh was neither begotten nor conceived through physical lust or desire. This flesh, in his view was mortal and capable of the normal changes of life, yet it was without sin. Christ cleansed it for his own use.[10]

Anselm (1033–1109) taught that Mary was sanctified, but not from her conception: his view was that Christ's mother was purified by the power of Christ's death.[11] It was his view that the Virgin Mary who bore Jesus could be pure only by true faith in His death. Thus her sanctification, as is true of all believers, could not have taken place until after Christ's passion.

Pareus (1548–1622) had a similar view of the sanctification and purification of Christ's flesh, rather than Mary's sinlessness. He wrote:

> It was not fitting for the Logos, the Son of God, to assume a nature polluted by sin. For whatever is born of flesh-that is, from a sinful, unsanctified woman, is flesh, falsehood, and worthlessness. The Holy Spirit well knew how to

separate sin from the nature of man, the substance from the accident. For sin is not the nature of the man but was added to the nature from somewhere else, by the devil. The Holy Spirit separated from the fetus all impurity and infection of original sin.[12]

Ursinius (1534–1583) wrote, "Mary was a sinner; but the mass of flesh which was taken out of her substance [the infant Jesus] was, by the operation of the Holy Spirit, at the same instant sanctified when it was taken."[13] A century later, Francis Turretin, also rejected the idea of the Immaculate Conception:

> The Holy Spirit must prepare the substance abscised from the substance of the blessed virgin by a suitable sanctification, not only by endowing it with life and elevating it to that degree of energy which is sufficient for generation without sexual connection, but also by purifying it from all stain of sin (*ab omni peccati labe*) so that it shall be harmless and undefiled, and thus that Christ may be born without sin. Hence there is no need of having recourse to the doctrine of the immaculate conception of Mary. For although there is no created power which can bring a clean thing from an unclean (Job 14:4), yet the divine power is not to be so limited. To this there is nothing impossible. This calls things which are not, as if they were.[14]

In his *Dogmatic Theology*, William Shedd explains the scriptural basis for recognizing that the flesh of Jesus was redeemed from original sin, but not the flesh of His mother. He writes:

> That the human nature derived from Mary in itself and apart from the agency of the Holy Spirit in the incarnation was corrupt is proved by Rom. 8:3: "God sent his own Son in the likeness of human flesh." This means that the "flesh" as it existed in the mother and before its sanctification in the womb was sinful. "That which is born of flesh is flesh"

(John 3:6); "who can bring a clean thing out of an unclean? Not one" (Job 14:4); "how can he be clean that is born of a woman?" (25:4). The Formula of Concord ("Concerning Original Sin," Hase 644) says that "in the first moment of our conception, that seed from which a man is formed is contaminated and corrupted by sin."[15]

Shedd gives scriptural evidence to show that all flesh is corrupt from the moment of conception and that for Jesus to be like us in every way, He had to take on that body of flesh. Yet before doing so, He purified the flesh that would be His body. Clearly, here there is no concept of the sinless nature of the mother of Jesus.

While the idea of the Immaculate Conception was popular in the Catholic Church even prior to its declaration as dogma, there were voices throughout the centuries that called for a more biblical understanding that Mary was equal to the rest of humanity but had the singular privilege of being the physical and familial mother of the Savior. This realistic and biblical view of Mary undercuts some of the reason for her veneration.

The second passage used to promote Marian veneration is Luke 1:42–43, Elizabeth's proclamation when she saw Mary: "Blessed are you among women, and blessed is the fruit of your womb! And how has it happened to me that the mother of my Lord would come to me?" The use of the word Lord in the phrase "mother of my Lord" refers to Jesus. The Greek *kyrios* is also used in the Shema: "Hear, O Israel: The Lord (*kyrios*) our God is one Lord." It is believed that this was the foundation for the decision to refer to Mary as mother of God to show that Jesus was both fully God and fully man (*homoousios*). However, as we saw in the story at the beginning of this book, Nestorius's concern that this title would elevate Mary to the status of a goddess among the uneducated laity was realized. Referring to Mary as the mother of God had the unintended effect of elevating her to virtual goddess status.

The subconscious desire of the people, from the earliest days, to have a goddess mirrored the desire of Old Testament Israel to have a king so that it could be like the other nations (1 Samuel 8:5). The syncretism that occurred around the time of Constantine continued the heart attitude that was first evidenced in Luke's Gospel by the woman who attempted to proclaim the blessedness of "the womb that bore you and the breasts at which you nursed" (Luke 11:27). We have seen that Jesus's response did not endorse this veneration of His mother. His reply that all those who hear and do the word of God are blessed certainly did include His mother, but not in the singular fashion taught by the Catholic Church.

The third passage that formed a basis for the elevation of Mary's place in the Catholic Church is Genesis 3:15, where God curses Satan for his role in the fall of man. God says, "And I will put enmity between you [Satan] and the woman [Eve], and between your seed and her seed; He [the seed, Jesus Christ] shall bruise you on the head, and you shall bruise Him on the heel." Taken literally, this is a clear reference to Eve and her posterity, the offspring of the "mother of all living" (Genesis 3:20). The bruising of the heel was Satan's temporary victory over Jesus when He was arrested and nailed to the cross. The reference to Christ bruising the head of Satan refers to Christ's complete victory over the results of Satan's actions in the Garden of Eden, which led to the death of mankind. Paul explained the effect of Christ's victory over Satan on the followers of Christ in his letter to the Colossians:

> When you were dead in your transgressions and the uncircumcision of your flesh, He [God] made you alive together with Him [Jesus Christ, resurrected], having forgiven us all our transgressions, having canceled out the certificate of debt consisting of decrees against us, which was hostile to us; and He [God] has taken it out of the way, having nailed it to the cross. (Colossians 2:13–24)

(We should note here that this was a "bruising" of the head of Satan, not his destruction. Though Christ overcame spiritual death, our bodies still die because Satan still lives. The complete and final victory of Christ over Satan and his dark forces will come at a future time. Romans 16:20 says, "The God of peace will soon crush Satan under your feet.") [16]

We have seen that Irenaeus was one of the first to make a connection between Eve and Mary. In *Proof of Apostolic Preaching* (circa 190), he wrote:

> And just as it was through a virgin who disobeyed [namely Eve] that mankind was stricken and fell and died, so too it was through the Virgin [Mary], who obeyed the word of God, that mankind, resuscitated by life, received life ... for Adam had necessarily to be restored in Christ, that morality be absorbed in immorality. And Eve [had necessarily to be restored] in Mary, that a virgin by becoming the advocate of a virgin, should undo and destroy virginal disobedience by virginal obedience.[17]

This sounds logical, but it is not supported by scripture. The apostle Paul, in writing to the Romans, gives us a clearer picture of the heritage of sin and death that began at the Fall.

> Therefore, just as through one man sin entered the world, and death through sin, and so death spread to all men, because all sinned ... Nevertheless death reigned ... even over those who had not sinned in the likeness of the offense of Adam, who is a type of him who was to come. But the free gift is not like the transgression. For if by the transgression of the one the many died, much more did the grace of God and the gift by the grace of the one Man, Jesus Christ, abound to the many. The gift is not like that which came through the one who sinned; for on the one hand the judgment arose from one transgression resulting in condemnation, but on the other hand the free gift arose from many transgressions resulting in justification. For if by the transgression of the one, death reigned through the one, much more those who receive the abundance of grace and of the gift of righteousness will reign in life through the One, Jesus Christ. So then as through one transgression there resulted condemnation to all men, even so through one act of righteousness there resulted justification of life to all men; for as through the one man's disobedience the many were made sinners, even through the obedience of the One the many will be made righteous. (Romans 5:12, 15–19)

Why Mary?

Paul emphasized this point again in his letter to the Corinthians, writing, "For as in Adam all die, so also in Christ all will be made alive" (1 Corinthians 15:22). These scriptures make it abundantly clear that sin entered the world through "one man's disobedience," which led to death, and that the only remedy necessary or possible is "the One, Jesus Christ."

While the account in Genesis does show that Eve succumbed to the deception and temptation of the serpent (Satan), scripture does not lay the burden of sin of disobedience solely on her, but on Adam. Although he had not been deceived, Adam willfully disobeyed the command given to him directly by God before Eve was even formed (Genesis 2:15–17). This is not because the man is more responsible, but because in God's eyes Adam represented the *adam*, i.e., man and woman joined together as "one flesh." We see this concept of "one flesh" in several places in scripture:

> The man said, "This is now bone of my bone and flesh of my flesh; she shall be called woman because she was taken out of man." For this reason a man shall leave his father and his mother and be joined to his wife; and they shall become one flesh. (Genesis 2:23–24)

> But from the beginning of creation, God made them male and female. For this reason a man shall leave his father and mother and the two shall become one flesh; so they are no longer two but one flesh. (Mark 10:6–8)

> Or do you not know that the one who joins himself to a prostitute is one body with her? For He [God] says, "The two shall become one flesh." (1 Corinthians 6:16)

Scripture is clear that this sin is one of disobedience on the part of "one man," Adam. The abundance of grace and the gift of righteousness are made available to us as the result of the obedience of "one man," Jesus Christ, to die on the cross. Only His obedience and His willing sacrifice of himself are sufficient to pay the penalty for all the sins of mankind, not just that original sin. Mankind divided into male and female is represented by the "one man," Adam, who was disobedient. His punishment—death, both physical and spiritual, and separation from God—flows to all mankind. The "one man," Jesus Christ, represented all mankind in His obedience to die to pay the penalty for all sin. Whereas the payment is made for all, it is only effective for those who join with the body of Christ through confession of sin and faith in Jesus Christ as their Savior and Lord. In this true economy of salvation, there is no need for Mary to be the spiritual "mother of all living" because the Father who created Adam (male and female) through his Son is also the Father who ordains eternal life through that same Son.

Perpetual Virginity

There is no disagreement among Christian churches that Jesus was born of a virgin. This is clearly established in Scripture. Isaiah (circa BC 739–BC 690) prophesied that the Messiah, the Christ, the Savior of the world, would be born of a virgin: "Therefore the Lord Himself will give you a sign: Behold a virgin will be with child and will bear a son, and she will call His name Immanuel" (Isaiah 7:14). The fulfillment of this prophecy is recorded in two gospels, Matthew and Luke.

> Now the birth of Jesus Christ was as follows: when His mother Mary had been betrothed (promised in marriage) to Joseph, before they came together she was found to be with child by the Holy Spirit. And Joseph her husband, being a righteous man and not wanting to disgrace her, planned to send her away secretly. But when he had considered this, behold, an angel of the Lord appeared to him in a dream, saying, "Joseph, son of David, do not be afraid to take Mary as your wife; for the Child who has been conceived in her is of the Holy Spirit. [21] She will bear a Son; and you shall call His name Jesus, for He will save His people from their sins." [22] Now all this took place to fulfill what was spoken by the Lord through the prophet (Isaiah): "Behold, the virgin shall be with child and shall bear a Son, and they shall call His name Immanuel," which translated means "God With Us." And Joseph awoke from his sleep and did as the angel of the Lord commanded

him, and took Mary as his wife, but kept her a virgin until she gave birth to a Son; and he called His name Jesus. (Matthew 1:18–25)

Now in the sixth month [of Elizabeth's pregnancy with John the Baptist] the angel Gabriel was sent from God to a city in Galilee called Nazareth, to a virgin engaged to a man whose name was Joseph, of the descendants of David; and the virgin's name was Mary. And coming in, he said to her, "Greetings, favored one! The Lord is with you." But she was very perplexed at this statement, and kept pondering what kind of salutation this was. The angel said to her, "Do not be afraid, Mary; for you have found favor with God. And behold, you will conceive in your womb and bear a son, and you shall name Him Jesus. He will be great and will be called the Son of the Most High; and the Lord God will give Him the throne of His father David; and He will reign over the house of Jacob forever, and His kingdom will have no end." Mary said to the angel, "How can this be, since I have known no man [am a virgin]?" The angel answered and said to her, "The Holy Spirit will come upon you, and the power of the Most High will overshadow you; and for that reason the holy Child shall be called the Son of God. And behold, even your relative Elizabeth has also conceived a son in her old age; and she who was called barren is now in her sixth month. For nothing will be impossible with God." And Mary said, "Behold, the bondslave of the Lord; may it be done to me according to your word." And the angel departed from her. (Luke 1:26–38)

Doctrine differs between Catholic and Protestant and evangelical churches on the Catholic dogma of the Perpetual Virginity of Mary. This dogma holds that Mary remained a virgin her entire life. *Catechism* teaches that Mary's virginity was preserved miraculously during the birth of Jesus.[18] Quoting Augustine, it goes on to state that Mary remained a virgin in the conception of her Son, in giving birth to Him, in carrying Him, and in nursing Him. She was always a virgin. When we looked at the history of Marian veneration, we saw what a great impact this idea had and still has on Catholic culture. The beginning of the monastic movement and the obsession of Pulcheria that profoundly influenced Marian veneration both had their roots in this doctrine. However, scripture does not support the perpetual virginity of Mary. More important for our purposes is the teaching that Mary never gave birth to any other children.[19] Gregg Allison, in his book *Roman Catholic Theology and Practice: An Evangelical Assessment*, explains the biblical teaching:

> But the idea that, in giving birth, Mary's virginity was preserved intact is not affirmed in Scripture; indeed, it is contradicted by the very simple and straightforward account of the event: "And she gave birth to her firstborn son and wrapped him in swaddling clothes and laid him in a manger, because there was no place for them in the inn" (Luke 2:7). There is no hint of a miraculous, virginity preserving intervention at Jesus's birth. What is more, after his birth, Mary did engage in sexual intercourse with Joseph, as described in Matthew (1:24–25): "He took his wife, but knew her not until she had given birth to a son." The word "until" (ἕως), used as a conjunction, indicates an end point to an ongoing state of things. That is, while Joseph did not engage in intercourse during the entire time … (which corresponded to the nine months of her pregnancy), they did so engage after the birth of Jesus. This fact is confirmed by references to Jesus being Mary's "firstborn son" (Luke 2:7), and to his brothers and sisters (Matt. 12:46 [par. Mark 3:31; Luke 8:19]; 13:55–56; Acts 1:14).[20]

In fact, three Gospel writers, Matthew, Mark, and John, as well as the apostle Paul, refer to the brethren of Jesus in language that attests to a strong familial connection. The obvious and natural conclusion from these passages is that after the miraculous conception of Jesus by the power of the Holy Spirit, Mary and Joseph had other children of their own.

> While He was still speaking to the crowds, behold, His mother and brothers were standing outside, seeking to speak to Him. (Matthew 12:46)

> Is not this the carpenter's son? Is not His mother called Mary, and His brothers, James and Joseph and Simon and Judas? (Matthew 13:55)

> Then His mother and His brothers arrived, and standing outside they sent word to Him and called Him. (Mark 3:31)

> After this He went down to Capernaum, He and His mother and His brothers and His disciples; and they stayed there a few days. (John 2:12)

> Therefore His brothers said to Him, "Leave here and go into Judea, so that Your disciples also may see Your works which You are doing. For no one does anything in secret when he himself seeks to be known publicly. If You do these things, show Yourself to the world." For not even His brothers were believing in Him. (John 7:3–5)

> Do we not have a right to take along a believing wife, even as the rest of the apostles and the brothers of the Lord and Cephas? (1 Corinthians 12:35)

> But I did not see any other of the apostles except James, the Lord's brother. (Galatians 1:19)

Although the Catholic Church teaches the perpetual virginity of Mary, there is ample biblical evidence, both in eyewitness accounts and in use of Greek language—the word "until" (ἕως)—that Mary was blessed by God with other children after the birth of Jesus.

There appears to be a confirming biblical relationship to the idea that Mary had other children as replacements for the one (Jesus) she would have to give up to the purposes of God. Job was given seven sons and three daughters to replace the ones Satan destroyed with God's permission (Job 42:13). Naomi lost two sons but was given the blessing of being allowed to be nurse for her grandson, who the women of the village recognized as Naomi's son (Ruth 4:16). The account of Hannah, wife of Elkanah, tells how she prayed for a son with the promise that she would give him back to the Lord if he answered her prayers. God blessed Hannah with a son, Samuel, in answer to that prayer. Hannah kept her promise to God to deliver Samuel to the temple to serve the Lord. God rewarded Hannah's faithfulness by blessing her with other children, three sons and two daughters (1 Samuel 1:1–2:11, 18–21).

Back in the era in which Jesus was born, a woman experienced shame if she could not have a child, as demonstrated by the account of Elizabeth, John's mother. Luke relates that when she realized she was pregnant, she praised God for taking away her "reproach among people" (Luke 1:25). In the case of Mary's pregnancy, Joseph, unaware of the miraculous nature of her condition, believed that, culturally, he had only two options: divorce her publicly, as was mandatory, which likely would lead to her being stoned for adultery; or divorce Mary quietly, saving himself humiliation and possibly saving her life.[21] After he is told by an angel in a dream that the child is of the Holy Spirit, Joseph chose a third option and married her, thus essentially sharing the shame of the out-of-wedlock pregnancy.

In a culture where the chief function of women was to bear children, especially sons,[22] pregnancy was seen as a blessing of God and barrenness as a curse. For Mary to have had no other children would have been seen as God's judgment on her (and Joseph because he married her, an indication of his complicity in the conception) for her perceived immoral behavior. However, for Mary to bear additional children would have been seen as a blessing from God; the shame would have faded over time. For God to bless Mary with other children was in keeping with His attribute of justice. Shedd explains that while God is under no obligation to reward his creatures, He is a just God.

> The exercise of remunerative justice by God is practical and gracious. It results from a previous covenant upon his part. The reward of a creature's obedience is in consequence of a

> divine promise ... Because God has originated the powers and capacities of a creature from nothing, he is entitled to all the agency of these facilities without paying for it ... All that strict justice would require on the part of God ... is that he should not cause him to suffer. That he should go further than this and positively reward him ... is gracious treatment.[23]

Would God's strict justice have required Mary to suffer the lifelong cultural consequences of conceiving a child outside of marriage? Would His strict justice have required Joseph to share in that shame? Neither of these conform to the grace of God evidenced throughout Scripture. What we do see in Scripture is the grace of God shown to Mary: the brothers (and sisters) of Jesus are his half-siblings and subsequent children of the union of Mary and Joseph: "Children are a gift of the Lord. The fruit of the womb is His reward" (Psalm 127:3).

The idea of the perpetual virginity of Mary follows very closely the ancient beliefs connected to goddess worship. As we saw in Pulcheria's story, the belief in the perpetual virginity of Mary, coupled with the ancient belief, inspired many to follow what they saw as Mary's example of a life of holiness whose earmark was a vow of celibacy. However, people do not have to accept the idea of Mary's perpetual virginity as a doctrine to live a celibate life based on their desire to wholeheartedly serve God. God promises a great reward for those who choose this life: "For thus says the Lord: 'To the [physical or spiritual] eunuchs who keep my Sabbaths, who choose the things that please me and hold fast my covenant, I will give in my house and within my walls a monument and a name better than sons and daughters; I will give them an everlasting name that shall not be cut off'" (Isaiah 56:3–5). Jesus said that some were born without sexual desire and some were castrated without their consent, but some chose to live this way for God (Matthew 19:12). Those who choose celibacy out of their desire to single-mindedly follow God are greatly blessed. Paul also spoke about this kind of life.

> Those who marry have worldly troubles ... I want you to be free from anxieties. The unmarried man is anxious about the things of the Lord, how to please the Lord. But

> the married man is anxious about worldly things, how to please his wife, and his interests are divided. And the unmarried or betrothed woman is anxious about the things of the Lord, how to be holy in body and spirit. But the married woman is anxious about worldly things, how to please her husband. I say this for your own benefit, not to lay any restraint upon you, but to promote good order and to secure your undivided devotion to the Lord. (1 Corinthians 7:28, 32–35)

It is not necessary to have Mary as a role model for a celibate life: God has provided that model, and evidence of its blessings, in His Word.

The Assumption

The assumption of Mary was proclaimed dogma by Pope Pius XII on November 1, 1950, in his encyclical *Munificentissimus Deus*. Yet there is no mention of the bodily assumption of Mary in either Scripture or in the writings of the early Christian church.

As mentioned above, Scripture provides accounts of two bodily assumptions that occurred while the people were still alive. Genesis 5:24 says, simply, that "Enoch walked with God and he was not, for God took him." What made Enoch so special that he did not have to face death? In the book of Jude, God suggests a reason:

> Enoch, in the seventh generation from Adam, prophesied, saying, "Behold, the Lord came with many thousands of His holy ones, to execute judgment upon all, and to convict all the ungodly of all their ungodly deeds which they have done in an ungodly way, and of all the harsh things which ungodly sinners have spoken against Him."

Enoch was not afraid to prophesy the truth of God's coming vengeance upon the people. He did not hesitate to speak out, even though what he had to say was unpopular and dangerous. Scripture does not give us more insight than these few verses.

Why Mary?

The other person to experience bodily assumption while still alive was the prophet Elijah. Second Kings 2:11 states that "Elijah went up by a whirlwind into heaven." Like Enoch, Elijah was a prophet who often said unpopular things. Yet, many other prophets also boldly spoke the Word of God and were martyred for it. Why then did God choose to take only these two? Scripture does not give us any definitive reasons. However, because scripture does give these accounts, it is curious that there is no mention of the bodily assumption of Mary.

The earliest mention of the death of Mary was by Cyril of Jerusalem, who wrote about the legendary account of a Jewish mob attempting to mutilate Mary's body during the funeral procession. Cyril gives no account of the assumption.[24] There are two legendary accounts of the death and assumption of Mary, supposedly by Bishop Evodius of either Rome or Antioch, and the apostle John, but these are word-of-mouth accounts only.

Explicit mention of the assumption of Mary does not appear until the fourth century. It is found in a letter from Juvenalius, patriarch of Jerusalem, to Empress Pulcheria, who was seeking relics of the Virgin Mary to be housed in the churches she was building. Juvenalius had attended the Council in Ephesus and was familiar with Pulcheria's power. He had seen firsthand the result of Nestorius's effort to correct Pulcheria's conception of the place and role of Mary in the Church. Juvenalius was aware that there was not any clear evidence about the place of Mary's death—either in Ephesus, where she lived with the apostle John, or in Jerusalem, as was rumored. He also knew that telling Pulcheria that no one knew Mary's resting place would not endear him to that powerful woman. He was already fighting for recognition of the legitimacy of his position alongside the bishops of Rome and Constantinople. To diffuse the situation, he wrote that he was surprised she did not know about the "ancient tradition" of the bodily assumption of the Virgin Mary after her death. Along with his letter he included an account alleging that the apostles had been assembled for the burial of Mary and that when the tomb was opened, her body was not there. Pulcheria had no choice but to accept this account as fact, as it came from one of the bishops of the Church and was reported to be part of church tradition. The letter, preserved by John of Damascus, has been cited as testimony to the assumption of Mary even though there is no specific Scriptural endorsement of its contents.[25]

Of the four dogmas, only Divine Motherhood—that Jesus was to be born of a virgin and that the virgin's name was Mary—is clearly supported in Scripture. The other three—the Immaculate Conception, Perpetual Virginity and the Assumption—have no clear scriptural basis. In fact, there is Scriptural basis to reject two of them. It is also historical fact that while these beliefs about Mary were commonly held by many people as early as the third century, none was formally endorsed by the Catholic Church until relatively recently. The circumstances that finally drove people to cry out for their endorsement were the apparitions of Mary that occurred in the late nineteenth and early twentieth centuries.

Chapter 21

Of the four dogmas associated with Mary, it is the Assumption that helps set the stage for the Catholic Church's support of the visions of Mary. Church officials reason that if Mary is present bodily in heaven, is it not probable that she might appear to the faithful here from time to time? Yet these appearances, while they appear to be heavenly, have much about them that is contrary to Scripture. We will consider the biblical implications of those appearances of the Virgin Mary that have had an impact on the four dogmas. These will be addressed in chronological order, beginning with the vision seen by Catherine Laboure of Paris.

As we have seen earlier, the vision of the Virgin Mary instructed Catherine Laboure to have a medal made according to the model she would see. The vision changed and, according Catherine, became Mary in a white dress with a blue mantle and a white veil. She was standing on a globe that had the year 1830 on its base. Rays of light extended from her downward stretched hands to cover the globe. One foot was on the head of a serpent. An oval formed around her, inscribed with the words "O Mary conceived without sin, pray for us who have recourse to thee." The apparition turned and Catherine saw what was to be the reverse of the medal: the letter M under a bar and a cross. Under the letter M were two hearts, one crowned with thorns (representing Jesus) and one pierced with a sword (representing Mary). Around this image was a circle of twelve stars. Catherine was told that those who wore the medal "with confidence" would receive "great graces."

Catherine had this same vision several more times and reported it to her priest, each time giving him the instructions she had received from the apparition regarding the medal. The priest did not believe her and this led to many disagreements between them. In 1832, the priest finally visited the archbishop of Paris, who embraced the idea of the medal and in June of that year produced 1,500 of them. By 1836, more than two million medals had been sold, and people were attributing miracles of cures, wonders, and death-bed conversions to the medals. As a result, there was a popular outcry to have the Immaculate Conception acknowledged as dogma, which led Pope Pius IX to issue the *Ineffabilis Deus*.

If we look at Catherine's visions and the direction given to her from a biblical viewpoint, we see much to indicate that this was not a God-ordained vision similar to those recorded in Scripture. The *Ineffabilis Deus* also contained language that was inconsistent with the Word of God. We will look at the parts of the vision, and its result, which are counter to Scripture.

First, the apparition told Catherine that the rays of light extending from her hands represented "the graces which I shed on those who ask me." The oval frame that appeared contained the words "O Mary, conceived without sin, pray for us who have recourse to you."[1] These would indicate an expectation that prayer for grace should be directed to Mary. As we have already addressed Scripture that refutes the concept of the sinlessness of Mary, we will consider how these aspects of the vision led to the declaration in the *Ineffabilis Deus* that "no one can come to the Father on high except through the Son, so almost in like manner, no one can come to Christ except through His Mother."[2] The vision also generated the papal statement that no one receives the redemptive grace of Christ without the intercessory cooperation of Mary. These two things—intercessory prayer to Mary and the idea that all grace flows through Mary—are not what Scripture teaches. In fact, Scripture is clear in regard to prayer and grace.

When the disciples of Jesus asked Him how they were to pray, Jesus gave them the model of the Lord's Prayer. This prayer, recorded in Matthew 6:9–13, teaches us to direct our prayer to God, "our Father," in heaven. This instruction is repeated in two places in the book of James.

> But if any of you lacks wisdom, let him ask of God, who gives to all generously and without reproach, and it will be given to him (James 1:5).

> Every good gift and every perfect gift is from above, coming down from the Father of lights, with whom there is no variation or shadow due to change (James 1:17).

Jesus also taught His disciples, and through His Word, us, that we are to ask the Father in the name of the Son, Jesus.

> Whatever you ask in my name, that will I do, so that the Father may be glorified in the Son. If you ask me anything in my name, I will do it (John 14:13–14).

> Truly, truly, I say to you, if you ask the Father for anything in my name, He will give it to you. Until now you have asked for nothing in my name; ask and you will receive, so that your joy may be made full (John 16:23–24).

Jesus clarified that we are not to ask Him to intercede for us but rather that we are to pray directly to God, our Father, through the authority given to us by Jesus.

> In that day you will ask in my name, and I do not say to you that I will request of the Father on your behalf; for the Father Himself loves you, because you have loved me and have believed that I came forth from the Father (John 16:26–27).

If Jesus taught that we were not to ask Him to intercede for us to the Father, why would Mary instruct anyone to ask her to intercede with her Son for us? And if we are to pray to the Father directly, as Jesus teaches, why would prayer to Mary even be necessary? A thorough reading of the Old and New Testaments clearly shows the model of praying to God the Father. Prayers of thanksgiving to Jesus for His sacrifice and prayers to Jesus and to the Holy Spirit for their presence in our lives are appropriate, certainly. But the focus of most of our prayers of adoration, confession, thanksgiving, and supplication (petition) should be to the Father in the name of the Son, our Lord Jesus Christ. Petition to any other entity in heaven is never suggested or implied.

The vision showed Mary dispensing grace over the world's population.

Whereas the papal decree acknowledged that people are not obligated to ask Mary for grace, it did instruct that no one receives the redemptive grace of Christ without the intercessory cooperation of Mary. This is also not taught in Scripture. In fact, Scripture is very clear about the origin and pathway of God's grace.

> Paul, a bond-servant of Christ Jesus, called as an apostle, set apart for the gospel of God, which He promised beforehand through His prophets in the holy Scriptures, concerning His Son, who was born of a descendant of David according to the flesh, who was declared the Son of God with power by the resurrection from the dead, according to the Spirit of holiness, *Jesus Christ our Lord, through whom we have received grace* and apostleship to bring about the obedience of faith among all the Gentiles for His name's sake (Romans 1:1–5).

> But now apart from the Law the righteousness of God has been manifested, being witnessed by the Law and the Prophets, even the righteousness of God through faith in Jesus Christ for all those who believe; for there is no distinction; for all have sinned and fall short of the glory of God, being justified as a gift *by His grace through the redemption which is in* Christ Jesus (Romans 3:21–24).

> For *by grace you have been saved through faith*; and that not of yourselves, it is the gift of God; not as a result of works, so that no one may boast (Ephesians 2:8–9).

> But to each one of *us grace was given according to the measure of* Christ's gift. (Ephesians 4:7)

> But we believe that *we are saved through the grace of the Lord Jesus*, in the same way as they also are" (spoken by Peter); recorded in Acts 15:11).

> (Italics added by the author.)

The voice of the apparition instructed Catherine that a medal was to be struck according to the model she was seeing and that this medal, when worn, would obtain great graces for those who wore it with confidence. Would a message from a supposedly heavenly being contradict the commandment of God in the Word of God? The Old Testament clearly states God's command against the practice of using any image when worshipping Him and His righteous anger against those who disobey.

> You shall not make for yourself an idol, *or any likeness* of what is in heaven above or on the earth beneath or in the water under the earth. You shall not worship them or serve them; for I, the Lord your God, am a jealous God, visiting the iniquity of the fathers on the children, on the third and the fourth generations of those who hate Me, but showing lovingkindness to thousands, to those who love Me and keep My commandments (Exodus 20:4–6; *italics added*).

> So watch yourselves, that you do not forget the covenant of the Lord your God which He made with you, and make for yourselves a graven image in the form of anything against which the Lord your God has commanded you. For the Lord your God is a consuming fire, a jealous God (Deuteronomy 4:23–24).

> For you shall not worship any other god, for the Lord, whose name is Jealous, is a jealous God (Exodus 34:14).

> So watch yourselves carefully, since you did not see any form on the day the Lord spoke to you at Horeb from the midst of the fire, so that you do not act corruptly and make a graven image for yourselves in the form of any figure, the likeness of male or female (Deuteronomy 4:16–18).

> You shall not make for yourselves idols, nor shall you set up for yourselves an image or a sacred pillar, nor shall you

> place a figured stone in your land to bow down to it; for I am the Lord your God (Leviticus 26:1).
>
> Let all those be ashamed who serve graven images, who boast themselves of idols; Worship Him (Psalm 97:7).

It is true that the Catholic Church makes a distinction between the worship due God the Father and the Son and the hyperdulia due to Mary.³ But does God even allow this distinction? Scripture indicates that God neither recognizes nor approves of it. In Exodus 20:3, God commands, "You shall have no other gods before me." This translation appears to allow veneration of Mary as long as it is not equal to the worship due God. But does it? God led Moses to clarify His intent, saying, "You shall love the Lord your God with *all your* heart, with *all* your soul, and with *all* your might" (Deuteronomy 6:5; *italics added*). God's intent was so important that it was clarified by Jesus Himself in the New Testament by both Matthew and Luke.

> One of them, an expert in the law, tested him with this question: "Teacher, which is the greatest commandment in the Law?" Jesus replied: "'Love the Lord your God with all your heart and with all your soul and with all your mind.' This is the first and greatest commandment" (Matthew 22:35–38).

When one is obedient to God's command to love Him with all of one's heart, soul, mind, and strength, there is no room for any type of adoration of any other being or creature in heaven or on the earth. Scripture is clear that bowing before, kneeling before, showing reverence to, or praying to anyone other than God is not acceptable. This includes giving credit for any miracles of any kind, including healing. Yet, when this medal was struck, following the instructions of the apparition, that is exactly what happened. Hilda Graef writes:

> The tremendous popularity of the medal, to which soon numerous miracles were attributed, had also a great influence on the definition of the Immaculate Conception,

as it impressed the doctrine on the consciousness of Catholic people and led to a growing demand to have it [the doctrine] solemnly defined.⁴

That definition was the *Ineffabilis Deus*.

There is one other aspect of the medal that we should consider in light of these scriptures. The apparition showed the reverse side of the medal as displaying the letter M (for Mary) surmounted with a bar and a cross under which there were two hearts, side by side—one with thorns depicting Christ, and the other with a sword depicting Mary. The prominence of the letter M and the side-by-side placement of the two hearts led to these pronouncements in the *Ineffabilis Deus*:

> The Feast of the Conception (of the Blessed Virgin) should be celebrated in every church with the very same honor as the Feast of the Nativity ... All our hope do we repose in the most Blessed Virgin—in the all fair and immaculate one who has crushed the poisonous head of the most cruel serpent and brought salvation to the world: in her who is the glory of the prophets and apostles, the honor of the martyrs, the crown and joy of all the saints; in her who is the safest refuge and the most trustworthy helper of all who are in danger; in her who, with her only-begotten Son, is the most powerful Mediatrix and Conciliatrix in the whole world; in her who is the most excellent glory, ornament, and impregnable stronghold of the holy Church; in her who has destroyed all heresies and snatched the faithful people and nations from all kinds of direst calamities; in her do we hope who has delivered us from so many threatening dangers. We have, therefore, a very certain hope and complete confidence that the most Blessed Virgin will ensure by her most powerful patronage that all difficulties be removed and all errors dissipated, so that our Holy Mother the Catholic Church may flourish daily more and more throughout all the nations and countries, and may reign "from sea to sea and from the river to the ends of the earth," and may enjoy

> genuine peace, tranquility and liberty. We are firm in our confidence that she will obtain pardon for the sinner, health for the sick, strength of heart for the weak, consolation for the afflicted, help for those in danger; that she will remove spiritual blindness from all who are in error, so that they may return to the path of truth and justice, and that here may be one flock and one shepherd.⁵

Does this communicate the same worship of God that Scripture tells us God requires? It does not. God does not share His glory with anyone.

> I am the LORD; that is my name! I will not give my glory to anyone else, nor share my praise with carved idols (Isaiah 42:8).

John, having been given the Revelation of Jesus Christ (concerning the end times) by God's heavenly messenger, was overwhelmed. Yet even he received this chastisement.

> Then I fell down at his feet to worship him [God's messenger], but he said, "No, don't worship me. I am a servant of God, just like you and your brothers and sisters who testify about their faith in Jesus. Worship only God. For the essence of prophecy is to give a clear witness for Jesus" (Revelation 19:10).

The message Catherine Laboure received from the apparition contains much that is contrary to the revealed Word of God. This message endorsed some key beliefs held by many people. Although the Catholic Church had embraced these beliefs in practice, the Magisterium had resisted the temptation to formalize them as dogma for centuries. The visions of the late nineteenth century changed that.

The visions of Bernadette Soubirous in 1858 have some of the same conflicts with Scripture. Bernadette told people that the apparition looked like one of the statues in her church, except she was "alive and surrounded by light." When she asked the apparition its name, the reply was, "I am the

Immaculate Conception." Bernadette was then instructed to have a chapel built on the site. After the visions ceased, Bernadette spent her life in a convent where she suffered physically and spiritually.

What are the scriptural responses to this vision? As to the figure of light's resemblance to one of the statues on the church, we read:

> For such people are false apostles, deceitful workers, masquerading as apostles of Christ. And no wonder, for *Satan himself masquerades as an angel of light* (2 Corinthians 11:14–15).
>
> I am amazed that you are so quickly deserting Him who called you by the grace of Christ, for a different gospel; which is really not another; only there are some who are disturbing you and want to distort the gospel of Christ. But even if we, *or an angel from heaven*, should preach to you a gospel contrary to what we have preached to you, he is to be accursed (Galatians 1:6–8).

(Italics added by the author.)

The apparition gives its name as the Immaculate Conception. We discussed in the chapter on dogma the biblical reasons that this title is not possible for Mary. So how can a seemingly miraculous vision use this name? Here is what Jesus said:

> Why do you not understand what I am saying? It is because you cannot hear My word. You are of your father *the devil*, and you want to do the desires of your father. He was a murderer from the beginning, and does not stand in the truth because there is no truth in him. *Whenever he speaks a lie, he speaks from his own nature, for he is a liar and the father of lies* (John 8:43–44; italics added).

The apparition told Bernadette to have a chapel built on the site. Scripture gives an account of Peter wanting to do the same thing after his encounter with Jesus, Moses and Elijah on the Mount of Transfiguration, and God's response.

> Six days later Jesus took with Him Peter and James and John his brother, and led them up on a high mountain by themselves. And He was transfigured before them; and His face shone like the sun, and His garments became as white as light. And behold, Moses and Elijah appeared to them, talking with Him. Peter said to Jesus, "Lord, it is good for us to be here; if You wish, I will make three tabernacles here, one for you, and one for Moses, and one for Elijah." While he was still speaking, a bright cloud overshadowed them, and behold, a voice out of the cloud said, "This is My beloved Son, with whom I am well pleased; listen to Him!" (Matthew 17:1–5).

God clearly rejected Peter's idea of building chapels to honor these biblical figures. God has allowed the building of houses of worship so that we might have the blessing of worshipping Him together, but these are for us, not God. Scripture shows us God's heart regarding the building of churches and chapels.

> David found favor in God's sight, and asked that he might find a dwelling place for the God of Jacob. But it was Solomon who built a house for Him. However, the Most High does not dwell in houses made by human hands; as the prophet says: "Heaven is My throne, and the earth is the footstool of My feet; what kind of house will you build for Me?" says the Lord, "Or what place is there for My repose? Was it not My hand which made all these things?" (Acts 7:46–50; Isaiah 66:1–2a).

If God does not desire a building, why would a lesser inhabitant of heaven request one? Jesus never requested a chapel be made for Him. One cannot think that Mary would raise herself above the level of her Son. But there is one spiritual being who does seek to be worshipped: Satan. The devil's desire for worship was made clear when he tempted Jesus in the wilderness.

> Again, the devil took Him to a very high mountain and showed Him all the kingdoms of the world and their glory; and he said to Him, "All these things I will give you, if you fall down and worship me." Then Jesus said to him, "Go, Satan! For it is written, 'You shall worship the LORD your God, and serve Him only'" (Matthew 4:8–10; Deuteronomy 6:13).

The 1846 vision seen by Melanie Calvat and Maximum Giraud had similar Scriptural inconsistencies. According to Melanie's account, the vision said two things that are particularly questionable. The vision said that she had the burden of continually praying for people so her Son would not abandon them. This directly contradicts God's own words, in both the Old and New Testaments, to those who follow Him.

> Be strong and courageous, do not be afraid or tremble at them, for the Lord your God is the one who goes with you. He will not fail you or forsake you ... The Lord is the one who goes ahead of you; He will be with you. He will not fail you or forsake you. Do not fear or be dismayed (Deuteronomy 31:6, 8).

> [Jesus said,] "Lo, I am with you always, even to the end of the age" (Matthew 28:20).

> Jesus answered them ... "My sheep hear my voice, and I know them, and they follow me; and I give eternal life to them, and they will never perish; and no one will snatch them out of my hand. My Father, who has given them to me, is greater than all; and no one is able to snatch them out of the Father's hand" (John 10:25, 27–29).

According to Melanie, the vision also said, "I gave you six days to work, I kept the seventh for myself, and no one wishes to grant it to me." Note that the apparition of Mary does not credit creation to God but to itself and claims the privilege of Sabbath worship as well. Whereas Jesus, as God, could say something of this nature, Mary is neither God nor part of the Trinity. No one who truly loves God would ever lay claim to what belongs to God alone.

> By the seventh day God completed His work which He had done, and He rested on the seventh day from all His work which He had done. Then God blessed the seventh day and sanctified it, because in it He rested from all His work which God had created and made (Genesis 2:2–3).

> Six days you shall labor and do all your work, but the seventh day is a sabbath of the Lord your God; in it you shall not do any work, you or your son or your daughter, your male or your female servant or your cattle or your sojourner who stays with you. For in six days the Lord made the heavens and the earth, the sea and all that is in them, and rested on the seventh day; therefore the Lord blessed the Sabbath day and made it holy (Exodus 20:9–11).

> Jesus said to them, "The Sabbath was made for man, and not man for the Sabbath" (Mark 2:27).

> For the Son of Man [Jesus] is Lord of the Sabbath (Matthew 12:8).

The Catholic Church has officially recognized nine major Marian apparitions. In each one where the apparition has spoken, we find contradictions to Scripture. At Fatima, there was an instruction to pray the Rosary, which repetitively calls on Mary for intercessory prayer. As we have seen, this is not biblical. The apparition in Beauraing, Belgium, called itself the Immaculate Virgin, Mother of God, and Queen of Heaven. The first two we have already addressed. The worship of the queen of heaven by God's chosen people, the Israelites, was condemned by God and incurred harsh judgment.

The children gather wood, and the fathers kindle the fire, and the women knead dough to make cakes for the *queen of heaven*; and they pour out drink offerings to other gods in order to spite me. "Do they spite me?" declares the Lord. "Is it not themselves they spite, their own shame?" Therefore thus says the Lord God, "Behold, my anger and my wrath will be poured out on this place, on man and on beast and on the trees of the field and on the fruit of the ground; and it will burn and not be quenched" (Jeremiah 7:18–20).

Then Jeremiah said to all the people, including all the women, "Hear the word of the Lord, all Judah who are in the land of Egypt, thus says the Lord of hosts, the God of Israel, as follows: 'As for you and your wives, you have spoken with your mouths and fulfilled with your hands, saying, "We will certainly perform our vows that we have vowed, to burn sacrifices to the *queen of heaven* and pour out drink offerings to her." Go ahead and confirm your vows, and certainly perform your vows!' Nevertheless hear the word of the Lord, all Judah who are living in the land of Egypt, 'Behold, I have sworn by my great name,' says the Lord, 'never shall my name be invoked again by the mouth of any man of Judah in all the land of Egypt, saying, "As the Lord God lives." Behold, I am watching over them for harm and not for good, and all the men of Judah who are in the land of Egypt will meet their end by the sword and by famine until they are completely gone. Those who escape the sword will return out of the land of Egypt to the land of Judah few in number. Then all the remnant of Judah who have gone to the land of Egypt to reside there will know whose word will stand, mine or theirs. This will be the sign to you,' declares the Lord, 'that I am going to punish you in this place, so that you may know that my words will surely stand against you for harm' (Jeremiah 44:24–29; *italics added*).

The pronouncements of these visions had great impact on the Catholic Church. Official recognition of the sightings of the apparitions and the apparitions' instructions directly resulted in the pronouncement of Church dogmas concerning the Virgin Mary: formal recognition the Church had resisted for centuries. How could these messages have had such a powerful impact when so much about them is contrary to God's own Word? Scripture itself gives us the answer:

> Now the Spirit expressly says that in later times some will depart from the faith by devoting themselves to deceitful spirits and teachings of demons (1 Timothy 4:1).
>
> For the time is coming when people will not endure sound teaching, but having itching ears they will accumulate for themselves teachers to suit their own passions, and will turn away from listening to the truth and wander off into myths (2 Timothy 4:3–4).

Hundreds of millions of people throughout the world have prayed to Mary in one of the various forms presented by the apparitions. Are you one of these people? Do you hear God calling you to lay aside your devotion to Mary and respond to His command to love Him with all of your heart, soul, mind, and strength? Do you understand that God wants *nothing* to stand between you and a personal relationship with Him?

Just before He went to the cross to pay for our sins, Jesus prayed for His disciples *and for you.*

> I do not ask on behalf of these alone, but for those also who believe in me through their word; that they may all be one; even as you, Father, are in me and I in you, that they also may be in us, so that the world may believe that you sent me. The glory which you have given me I have given to them, that they may be one, just as we are one; I in them and you in me, that they may be perfected in unity, so that the world may know that you sent me, and loved them, even as you have loved me. Father, I desire that they

also, whom you have given me, be with me where I am, so that they may see my glory which you have given me, for you loved me before the foundation of the world (John 17:20–24).

This passage speaks of the intimate relationship Jesus Christ has with the Father. Jesus prays that each one of those who believe that He is the Son of God will have that same intimate relationship with the Trinity—the complete unity of the body of Christ interacting with the Father and Son with nothing standing in the way. Jesus wants to have that personal relationship with every living person, including you. He said: "Behold, I stand at the door and knock; if anyone hears my voice and opens the door, I will come in to him and will dine with him, and he with me" (Revelation 3:20).

Part IV

Why Jesus

Chapter 22

Do you see that God does not want separation between you and a personal relationship with Him through His Son, Jesus?

Before Jesus died on the cross to pay the penalty for our sins, there had to be separation between God and man. In Genesis, we see how the intimate relationship God had with Adam and Eve was broken. God did choose some with whom He spoke directly. Most notably was Moses of whom the Bible says, "Thus the Lord used to speak to Moses face to face, just as a man speaks to his friend" (Exodus 33:11). But when God gave Moses the model for the tabernacle, and later when God gave King David the model for the temple in Jerusalem, there was a veil separating God from His people. Only the high priest was permitted to pass through that veil, and then only once per year after sacrifice had been made for the sins of the nation and for the sins of the priests.

Scripture tells us that the moment Jesus died on the cross to pay the penalty for our sins, God removed that barrier: "And Jesus cried out again with a loud voice, and yielded up His spirit. And behold, the veil of the temple was torn in two from top to bottom" (Matthew 27:50–51).

The suffering and death of Jesus, the Son of God, on the cross paid the penalty for all of the sins of all men for all time. At the moment His victory over our sins was complete, the veil in the temple was torn by God's hand (top to bottom) so that His people would have direct access to Him. Just as the temple veil prevented people from direct access to the Holy of Holies, i.e., the presence of God, so too have you allowed the veil of Mary to come between you and an intimate, personal relationship with the God the Father and His Son, our Lord and Savior, Jesus Christ. It is time to remove that veil. Are you ready to let it go?

Sharon F. Lawlor

A Love Letter

Have you ever been truly, deeply in love? When you are truly in love, thoughts of your beloved are on your mind continually: the first thing you think of in the morning and the last in your thoughts as you fall asleep. Every moment of your day is enriched by thoughts of your loved one—how they would laugh at the antics of a playful puppy, how they would weep at a little child's suffering, how they would find joy in the exquisite colors of sunset after a storm. You make plans around things that please your love; you seek to know the heart of your beloved so your plans will mirror theirs. True love is all consuming. The Bible describes this love beautifully.

> Love is patient, love is kind and is not jealous; love does not brag and is not arrogant, does not act unbecomingly; it does not seek its own, is not provoked, does not take into account a wrong suffered, does not rejoice in unrighteousness, but rejoices with the truth; bears all things, believes all things, hopes all things, endures all things. Love never fails (1 Corinthians 13:4–7).

Of all the greatest love stories of all time, none can come close to the love story God wrote in the Bible. The Bible is not just a book. It is a love letter written to you. Your Father, God, loves you infinitely more than you can possibly imagine.

What makes this love so amazing is that God knows you intimately. He knows every thought and intent of your heart. He sees every deed, good and bad. He knows the true motivation behind every seemingly good deed, sometimes better than we know ourselves. Because of this knowledge, Scripture says, "All have sinned and fall short of the glory of God" (Romans 3:23). Yet, God loves you.

When God created humans, male and female, He had an intimate relationship with them. God made the Garden of Eden to please His beloved. God walked with Adam and Eve in the garden because He loved spending time with them. God spoke to them, and they responded because they loved God. God gave them work, and they were obedient because they wanted to please Him.

Why Mary?

That intimacy was precious to God, but it was also fragile. It was fragile because while God's love was based on God's perfection, Adam and Eve were not perfect. For the love of man to be meaningful, it had to be intentional. For man's love to be intentional, it had to be his choice. It was for this reason that God placed one tree in the garden that was forbidden. Not the entire tree; they could still enjoy its beauty and its shade. Only the fruit of the tree was forbidden. It was a simple thing, really. Adam and Eve had abundance, for that is what love does, isn't it? Love provides abundantly.

Why does someone turn away from true love? If you had everything your heart could desire, would you turn your back on it? If God loved Adam and Eve so much, why would He place even one small thing in the garden and say it was forbidden? It is because for love to be true, it must be two-sided. You cannot force someone to love you. If you made a robot that looked and acted just like a real person and programmed it to love you, that love would not be satisfying. God wanted man to truly love Him and for that to happen, man had to have a choice.

If you are reading this book, you no doubt know what happened. Satan arrived in all his glory. Pictures of the garden show Satan as a snake, which is what he looked like after God punished him. But the Bible's description of Satan before he was cursed is altogether different.

> You had the seal of perfection, full of wisdom and perfect in beauty. You were in Eden, the garden of God; every precious stone was your covering: the ruby, the topaz and the diamond; the beryl, the onyx and the jasper; the lapis lazuli, the turquoise and the emerald; and the gold, the workmanship of your settings and sockets, was in you. On the day that you were created they were prepared. You were the anointed cherub who covers, and I placed you there (Ezekiel 28:12–14).

Satan was beautiful! Most likely, he was the most beautiful creature Adam and Eve had ever seen. Scripture does not tell us why they went near the forbidden tree on the day Satan appeared in Eden. But you can see why they were drawn to him.

Satan, this beautiful dragon, spoke to them. He caused them to doubt God's word. He caused them to doubt God's love.

> Now the serpent was more crafty than any beast of the field which the Lord God had made. And he said to the woman, "Indeed, has God said, 'You shall not eat from any tree of the garden'?" The woman said to the serpent, "From the fruit of the trees of the garden we may eat; but from the fruit of the tree which is in the middle of the garden, God has said, 'You shall not eat from it or touch it, or you will die.'" The serpent said to the woman, "You surely will not die! For God knows that in the day you eat from it your eyes will be opened, and you will be like God, knowing good and evil." When the woman saw that the tree was good for food, and that it was a delight to the eyes, and that the tree was desirable to make one wise, she took from its fruit and ate; and she gave also to her husband with her, and he ate. Then the eyes of both of them were opened, and they knew that they were naked; and they sewed fig leaves together and made themselves loin coverings (Genesis 3:1–7).

Adam and Eve were not tempted by a piece of forbidden fruit. They were tempted by something far greater and more wonderful. Although the love of God had been perfect and complete, it was forgotten in the presence of this magnificent creature. Adam gave names to every living thing in the garden, but he had never seen anything like this dragon. And that is how love dies. The one who completes you, the one who fulfills the desire of your heart, becomes unloved when your heart finds a new desire.

God did not leave Adam and Eve. God did not choose to sever His relationship with man. Remember, God knows everything we think, say, and do. God knew that Adam and Eve chose to believe Satan rather than Him. Because they chose to listen to Satan, they disobeyed the only rule God made. They ate the fruit.

Here is the all-surpassing wonderful grace of God: knowing they had rejected Him, God still came to the garden to spend time with them. God still hoped they would come to Him and ask forgiveness. God still hoped they would choose Him, even though He knew they would not.

Can you imagine the pain in God's heart when it was time to walk with Adam and Eve in the garden, and they didn't show up? God came. God called them. They didn't want to see God because they were ashamed. When God asked, lovingly, if they had eaten from the forbidden tree, He hoped they would so desire His love and presence that they would ask for His forgiveness. But they did not.

> They heard the sound of the Lord God walking in the garden in the cool of the day, and the man and his wife hid themselves from the presence of the Lord God among the trees of the garden. Then the Lord God called to the man, and said to him, "Where are you?" He said, "I heard the sound of you in the garden, and I was afraid because I was naked; so I hid myself." And He said, "Who told you that you were naked? Have you eaten from the tree of which I commanded you not to eat?" The man said, "The woman whom you gave to be with me, she gave me from the tree, and I ate." Then the Lord God said to the woman, "What is this you have done?" And the woman said, "The serpent deceived me, and I ate" (Genesis 3:8–12).

Adam blamed God for giving him Eve. Eve blamed the serpent. Neither Adam nor Eve sought God's forgiveness. Together they accepted God's punishment, never once begging God to forgive them. The Tree of Knowledge had made it possible for them to understand good and evil. Because they did not choose a relationship with God who is perfect goodness, they, by default, chose evil.

God gave them the result of their choice: they were cursed, sent from the garden, and forbidden access to the Tree of Life. Their ability to communicate directly with God, which was the presence of the Holy Spirit in their hearts, was removed. They died spiritually long before they died physically.

When we truly, deeply, love someone, we don't stop loving them because they reject us. Nor do we stop loving them when they hurt us. Why do you think this is? It is because God made us in His image. God's love never fails. The entire Bible is the story of God's effort to restore the intimate relationship He had with us, represented by Adam and Eve, in the garden. And oh, what lengths God has gone to in order to draw us to Himself!

> For God so loved the world [you!] that He gave His only begotten Son, that whoever believes in Him should not perish but have eternal life (John 3:16).

God is absolutely loving but also perfectly righteous and perfectly just. Adam and Eve endured punishment for rejecting God, but punishment was not God's goal. God's goal was a restored relationship. Even if man had asked for forgiveness, there would still have been a price to pay. Adam and Eve still would have to atone for the sin of rejecting God's love in order for the relationship with God to be restored.

God so desired relationship with man that he initiated a system of blood sacrifice. He told man that "life is in the blood" (Leviticus 17:11) and that "without the shedding of blood, there is no forgiveness" (Hebrews 9:22). The first blood shed was that of the animals God killed to provide a covering of skins for His children.

The problem with the system of blood sacrifice is twofold. First, man has to want God's love and forgiveness. Second, once the shedding of blood is accomplished, man has to turn his back on his sinful ways! Without the life-giving Sprit of God, man is not able to do either one. When man rejected God, God's Holy Spirit left his heart. In its place was emptiness. Because Adam and Eve chose to follow Satan's suggestions, they opened their hearts to his presence.

> And you were dead in your trespasses and sins, in which you formerly walked according to the course of this world, according to the prince of the power of the air [Satan], of the spirit that is now working in the sons of disobedience (Ephesians 2:1–2).

> And He [Jesus] was saying, "That which proceeds out of the man, that is what defiles the man. For from within,

out of the heart of men, proceed the evil thoughts, fornications, thefts, murders, adulteries, deeds of coveting and wickedness, as well as deceit, sensuality, envy, slander, pride and foolishness" (Mark 7:20–22).

It has been said that there are God-shaped holes in our hearts where the Spirit of God is meant to dwell. Because Adam and Eve rejected God, every person who is born has this hole. Because God allowed Satan to be the prince of this world, he sends his wicked spirits to dwell there. This is the spirit of disobedience that says, "No," to God. We see it in our own children; one of the first words they say is, "No."

Before God began His creation, He knew man would reject Him. God –the Father, the Son, and the Holy Spirit– planned, from before the creation of the world, for the Son to be the perfect, once-for-all sacrifice for sin. God planned for Christ's willing sacrifice to restore the relationship between Himself and man.

For His own blood to be shed, God had to become one of us. The Trinity agreed, and God sent the Son to become a man, born of a virgin. Fully God, Jesus was perfect and righteous in His nativity. Fully man, Jesus was filled with the Spirit of God and perfect and righteous in His obedience. Because Jesus was and is fully God and fully man, He alone lived a human life without sin. Jesus, the only begotten Son of God, was the perfect sacrifice needed to facilitate the restoration of the intimate relationship between God and man that God so desires because He loves us.

One thing remained. For God's sacrifice to be sufficient, it had to be done willingly, in full knowledge of all that it entailed. Jesus had to be not only fully man, enduring all physical and emotional pain man feels, but fully God, knowing every sin ever committed by man in order to suffer and die and pay the penalty for those sins.

It was this knowledge that Jesus dealt with in the garden of Gethsemane. This was the source of His agony. This is why He cried out, sweating drops of blood, "My Father, if it is possible, let this cup pass from me; yet not as I will, but as You will" (Matthew 26:39). Then after angels ministered to Him to give Him strength to accept the horrendous torment that He knew awaited Him, He was able to say, twice, "My Father, if this cannot pass away unless I drink it, Your will be done" (Matthew 26:39–42).

The Bible tells us in that man's just punishment for his sin is an eternity of torment in the lake of fire (Revelation 21:8) and eternal separation from God (2 Thessalonians 1:9). When Jesus was beaten and mocked on His way to Golgotha, it was just the beginning of the punishment He would endure on our behalf. Scripture tells us Jesus hung on the cross for three hours. During those three hours, darkness covered the land. What Jesus was suffering—the agony of the flames of the lake of fire for the sins of every man who would ever live—was so horrendous, God chose to hide it from sight. Creation could not bear to witness the horror and survive.

The perfect Lamb of God was the only sacrifice sufficient to pay that terrible debt. When Jesus proclaimed, "It is finished" (John 19:30), He meant that payment was complete. The death of Jesus paid the debt owed to God for all sin. Jesus's Resurrection was victory over our spiritual and physical death, and Jesus's Ascension into heaven opened the door for all who believe in Him to be joined with Him there. The intimate relationship between God and man was restored.

Jesus paid it all. There is no sin or guilt that was not covered by His blood. His blood was sufficient to pay the debt completely. If it were possible for the righteousness of any man or woman to pay part of the debt incurred, Jesus would not have had to suffer as He did. In fact He asked that very question of the Father! The answer was, "No." There was no other way.

The word God uses to describe the result of Jesus's obedience to suffer and die for us is "justification." This means that when we in faith believe that Jesus died on the cross to pay the penalty for our sins, and repent and embrace Him as Lord and Savior, God declares us "not guilty," based on the payment Jesus made. This justification is not only for past sins. When you love God with all of your heart, mind soul, and strength, you desire to please Him. When you are aware that that Jesus suffered on the cross to pay for your sins, you are very careful not to sin and cause Him more suffering. Because none of us is perfect, we will still sin. But when we belong to Jesus, a simple acknowledgement of our transgression to our Father, God, is sufficient, because in Christ we are fully justified, now and forever. It is not because of anything we do, but because of what Christ Jesus did on the cross.

God gave us a very clear explanation of the wonderful gift of justification that Jesus bought for us through His own suffering.

> Therefore, having been justified by faith, we have peace with God through our Lord Jesus Christ ... For while we were still helpless, at the right time Christ died for the ungodly ... God demonstrates His own love toward us, in that while we were yet sinners, Christ died for us. Much more then, having now been justified by His blood, we shall be saved from the wrath of God through Him ... Therefore, just as through one man sin entered into the world, and death through sin, and so death spread to all men, because all sinned ... But the free gift is not like the transgression. For if by the transgression of the one the many died, much more did the grace of God and the gift by the grace of the one Man, Jesus Christ, abound to the many. The gift is not like that which came through the one who sinned; for on the one hand the judgment arose from one resulting in condemnation, but on the other hand the free gift arose from many transgressions resulting in justification. For if by the transgression of the one, death reigned through the one, much more those who receive the abundance of grace and of the gift of righteousness will reign in life through the One, Jesus Christ ... For as through the one man's disobedience the many were made sinners, even so through the obedience of the One (Jesus) the many will be made righteous (Romans 5:1, 6, 8–9, 12, 15–17, 19).

In this passage, we see a reference to the one sin of man (Adam and Eve) and the many sins for which Jesus died. Here is why. In the Garden of Eden, God had only one law: do not eat from the Tree of Knowledge of Good and Evil that was in the center of the garden—only one law. When man disobeyed that one law, he broke every law that existed because there was only one.

Once man had an awareness of good and evil, God gave him many other laws. Jesus combined those laws into two basic precepts.

> "You shall love the Lord your God with all your heart, and with all your soul, and with all your mind." This is the great and foremost commandment. The second is like it, "You shall love your neighbor as yourself." On these two commandments depend the whole Law and the prophets (Matthew 22:36–40).

The Bible tells that that every person who ever lived transgressed against these two precepts, which contain all of the laws of God. Because there are many laws contained therein, there are many sins. Jesus died to pay them all.

This sacrifice of Jesus, the only perfect, spotless Lamb of God, was God's gift to us. Payment for our sins has been made. As with any gift, we need to take it, embrace it, and use it. We can only take this gift God has provided for each of us by confessing our sinfulness, intentionally turning away from sin, and giving our heart, soul, mind, and strength to God in love. We each do this when we ask Jesus to come into our heart and be our personal Lord and Savior.

The moment we choose to give our heart, soul, mind, and strength to Him, God sends the Holy Spirit to dwell in our heart to give us strength to follow Him. That God-shaped hole in our heart is filled with Him; Satan no longer has a dwelling place (though he will still attack from without). If we reject this gift, we must then pay the penalty of eternal separation from God in the lake of fire. How sad to endure torment that has already been paid!

Now that we know all that God has done out of His love for us, where does that leave Mary? If Jesus paid it all, there is no need for a doctrine that calls Mary co-redemptrix. If Jesus paid it all and stands before the Father on our behalf, where is the necessity of having Mary as mediatrix? In fact, Jesus warns against asking for Mary's intervention instead of praying to the Father in Jesus's name.

> Not everyone who says to me, "Lord, Lord" will enter the kingdom of heaven, but he who does the will of my Father who is in heaven. Many will say to me on that day, "Lord, Lord, did we not prophesy in your name, and in your name cast out demons, and in your name perform many miracles?" And then I will declare to them, "I never

knew you; depart from me, you who practice lawlessness" (Matthew 27:21–23).

What is the lawlessness Jesus is condemning? It is rejecting Jesus' sacrifice as full payment for all of your sins and the guilt associated with them. It is failing to love God with all of your heart, soul, mind, and strength. It is believing your works, or the righteous works of Mary or any other, can pay any part of the penalty for which Jesus has already atoned. To seek any of these other avenues of redemption is to reject Christ's sacrifice on your behalf. To reject Christ is to reject God. To reject God is the sin of Adam and Eve. The punishment is eternal separation from God.

Where are you today? If you have been deceived into believing there is any way to salvation and eternal life other than through the sacrifice of Christ, God already knows. What is God's goal? God loves you and wants to have that same intimate relationship with you that He had with your parents in the Garden of Eden. If they had told God they were sorry for what they had done, He would have forgiven them. He wants nothing more and nothing less from you.

Are you willing to give God, alone, all of your heart, soul, mind and strength?

Are you willing to fall at the feet of the Father, the Creator of all things, and ask His forgiveness in the name of His Son, Jesus?

Are you willing to thank Jesus, who loved you so much, he laid aside His throne and became a man and suffered and died to pay the penalty for your sins?

Are you willing to intentionally let go of your own plans and dreams and let the Holy Spirit come alive in you to give you spiritual life and God's direction?

If you humble yourself before the Lord God today and commit these things to God, He promises never to leave you or forsake you. He promises to give you eternal life with Him in heaven and abundant life with Him while you are here on the earth. While you are still here, there will be trials, heartaches, and rejection. But if you are faithful to your commitment to God, He will see you through every challenge, and each one will deepen your relationship with Him.

Do not wait. You do not know at what moment God will stop your breath. Your loving Father has waited all of your life to hear your voice. "If we confess our sins, He is faithful and righteous to forgive us our sins and to cleanse us from all unrighteousness (1 John 1:9).

No formal prayer is necessary. The Holy Spirit is here, waiting to help you know what to say. Prayer is just talking to God, telling Him what is in your heart. Start with, "Father God…."

Epilogue

If you prayed to God and poured out your heart to Him, asked for forgiveness for sin, and asked Jesus to come and dwell in your heart, be assured that God has heard it! As of this moment, the veil of sin separating you from God has been torn away—not because of anything you did, but because of what Jesus Christ did for you. You have been forgiven of your sins, including the sin of trusting in anything but Jesus, and Jesus promises never to leave you. In response to your faith in Christ alone, you have been given a brand new life, a spiritual life as a new child of God. God has breathed the Holy Spirit—the seal of eternal life—into your heart.

God has so much He wants to say to you now that you have chosen to have this intimate relationship with Him. It is all contained in His Word, the Bible. God promises that if you ask Him, He will help you understand it. All scriptures I used in this book are from the New American Standard translation. If you do not have access to that Bible, use the King James version, which is available almost everywhere.

Just as God created us to have fellowship with Him, He wants us to have fellowship with His other children who know Jesus as their personal Savior. If someone you know gave you this book, talk to this person first. Paul told us, "If you confess with your mouth Jesus as Lord, and believe in your heart that God raised Him from the dead, you will be saved" (Romans 10:9). Tell this person you have asked Jesus to be your Savior and that you have made the choice to love God with all of your heart, soul, mind, and strength.

If you do not have a Bible or someone you can talk to, you can find encouragement for your new life in Christ on the Internet. Log on to http://godlife.com/look-to-jesus, where you will find answers to any questions you may have. Even more important, you will find a real person somewhere in the world who is waiting to hear from you! God has already chosen the person who will help you grow in your faith. Just reach out.

Jesus has been praying for you (John 17:21–22). Jesus welcomes you by name into His Kingdom! The angels in heaven are rejoicing over you even now (Luke 15:10). Welcome home. God bless you as you seek to know Him and love Him ever more deeply.

References

Chapter 1

1. Holum, *Empresses*, 76.
2. Limberis, *Heiress*, 37.
3. Palladius, *Dialogus*, 108-9; Sozomen, *History*,8.17, 8.20, 8.27; Holum, *Empresses*, 77.
4. Holum, *Empresses*, 77.
5. Sozomen, *History*, 9.1; Holum, *Empresses*, 82; Eliott, "Protevangelium," in *Apocryphal*, pp. 48-67.
6. Holum, *Empresses*, 81-3; Limberis, *Heiress*, 41-3.
7. Holum, *Empresses*,84-7; Socrates, *History*, 7.1.
8. Holum, *Empresses*,81.

Chapter 2

1. Holum, *Empresses*, 88-90, 94-6.
2. Ibid, 81, 91, 94; Limberis, *Heiress*, 41.
3. Holum, *Empresses*, 90-2; Sozomen, *History*, 9.1.

Chapter 3

1. Limberis, *Heiress*, 92-6; Holum, *Empresses*, 90-2.
2. Sozomen, *History*, 9.1; Holum, *Empresses*, 93.
3. Holum, *Empresses*, 139.
4. Eliott, "Protevangelium," in *Apocryphal*, pp. 48-67.
5. Holum, *Empresses*, 92-6, 111,138-9, 141; Limberis, *Heiress*, 42-3; Socrates, *History*, 7.22;Sozomen, *History*, 9.1.
6. Holum, *Empresses*, 97.
7. Ibid, 97.

Chapter 4

1. Holum, *Empresses*, 97, 102-9,138-9; Limberis, *Heiress*, 42, 50-53; Sozomen, *History*, 9.3.
2. Holum, *Empresses*, 138-141; Socrates, *History*, 7.2.
3. Holum, *Empresses*, 97-9.
4. Limberis, *Heiress*, 94.
5. Holum, *Empresses*, 139.

Chapter 5

1. Holum, *Empresses*, 115-7, 120-1, 131, 133-4, 136-7.
2. Ibid,123-30.
3. Ibid, 125.

Chapter Six

1. Holum, *Empresses*, 140-146, 149.
2. Ibid, 139, 141; Socrates, *History*, 7.25, 7.26.
3. Holum, *Empresses*, 137-8.
4. Ibid, 134-6.
5. Ibid, 145-6.
6. Ibid, 144,148; Socrates, *History*, 7.26.
7. Holum, *Empresses*, 149-155; Limberis, *Heiress*, 53-57.
8. Holum, *Empresses*, 153.

Chapter Seven

1. Holum, *Empresses*, 149.
2. Ibid, 149-50.
3. Socrates, *History*, 7.29. 4-5.
4. Abramowski, *Nestorius*, 92; Holum, *Empresses*, 151.
5. Limberis, *Heiress*, 53-6; Holum, *Empresses*, 152.
6. Abramowski, *Nestorius*, 91-2; Holum, *Empresses*, 154.
7. Abramowski, *Nestorius*, 89; Holum, *Empresses*, 152-3.
8. Socrates, *History*,7.32.1-2.
9. Loofs, *Nestoriana*, 252.
10. Holum, *Empresses*, 154-5.
11. Ibid, 155.

12 Holum, *Empresses*, 155-6; Limberis, *Heiress*, 55-6; Graef, *Mary* (for more extensive quote of this sermon), 79-80.
13 Loofs, *Nestoriana*, 337-38.
14 Holum, *Empresses*, 157.
15 Holum, *Empresses*, 158; Loofs, *Nestoriana*, 165-182.
16 Holum, *Empresses*, 159-60.
17 Ibid, 161.
18 Holum, *Empresses*, 162-3; Graef, *Mary*, 80-4.
19 Holum, *Empresses*, 170-1.
20 Ibid, 176.

Chapter Eight

1   Holum, *Empresses*, 178.
2   Ibid.
3   Ibid, 177.
4   Ibid, 179.
5   Ibid, 180.
6   Socrates, *History*, 7.40.1-2.
7   Ibid, 7.44.
8   Holum, *Empresses*, 184.
9   Socrates, *History*, 7.45; Limberis, *Heiress*, 53.
10 Holum, *Empresses*, 188.
11 Ibid.
12 Ibid, 189.
13 Ibid, 192.
14 Ibid.
15 Ibid, 193-94.
16 Ibid, 199-200.
17 Ibid, 199.
18 Ibid, 201.
19 Ibid.
20 Ibid, 203.
21 Ibid, 204.
22 Ibid, 205.
23 Ibid, 206.
24 Ibid, 207.
25 Ibid, 208.
26 Ibid, 213.
27 Ibid.
28 Ibid, 215.

29 Ibid, 204.
30 Ibid, 215-16.

Part II

Chapter 9

1   Graef, *Mary*, 25-7.
2   Charles, *Isaiah*, 75.
3   Bernard, *Odes*, 86.
4   Graef, *Mary*,28.
5   Gambero, *Mary*, 44.
6   Justin, *Dialogue*, 78-9.
7   Elliott, "Protevangelium," 64-5.
8   Origin, *Commentary*, 956-57.
9   Gambero, *Mary*,79.
10 Graef, *Mary*, 34.
11 Gambero, *Mary*,104-5; Graef, *Mary*, 41-2.
12 Gambero, *Mary*, 76-8; Perry, *Mary*, 154-5.
13 Graef, *Mary*, 45.
14 Ibid, 44.
15 Gambero, *Mary*, 205, 214-5; Perry, *Mary*, 161-65.
16 Perry, *Mary*, 155-61

Chapter 10

1   Eusebius, *Constantine*, 4.24.
2   Malalas, *Chronographia*, 13.8
3   Limberis, *Heiress*,19.
4   Karweise, "Church," 311-20.

Chapter 11

1   Holum, *Empresses*, 16-7.
2   Ibid, 28.
3   Malalas, *Chronographia*, 13.39.
4   Holum, *Empresses*, 19.
5   Ibid, 22.
6   Ibid, 23-4.

7   Ibid, 20-21.
8   Ibid, 53-4.
9   Ibid, 55-6.
10 Ibid, 57.
11 Ibid, 62-3.
12 Ibid, 70.
13 Socrates, *History*, 6.11, 1-7, 11-21.
14 Holum. *Empresses*, 72.
15 Sozomen, *History*, 8.13.5.
16 Socrates, *History*, 6.15, 1-4; Sozomen, *History*, 8.16, 1-2.
17 Holum, *Empresses*, 74-5.
18 Socrates, *History*, 6.16, 1-5; Sozomen, *History*, 8.18, 1-4.
19 Sozomen, *History*, 8.20; Holum, 76-7; Limberis, *Heiress*, 37-8.
20 Holum, *Empresses*, 77.

Chapter 12

1   Karweise, *Ephesos*, 311-20.
2   Rubin, *Mother*, 63-4.
3   Pelikan, *Mary*, 77.
4   Limberis, *Heiress*, 60.
5   Ibid, 68.
6   Ibid, 89.
7   Limberis, *Heiress*, 89; Graef, *Mary*, 101.
8   Graef, *Mary*, 100-01.

Chapter 13

1   Rubin, *Mother*, 98; Graef, *Mary*, 113.
2   Graef, *Mary*, 113-5.
3   Ibid, 117-9.
4   Ibid, 119-25; Perry, *Mary*, 172-4.
5   Graef, *Mary*, 127-9; Perry, *Mary*, 177-80.
6   Graef, *Mary*, 129-33.
7   Ibid, 133-4.
8   Ibid, 143.
9   Ibid, 154-6.
10 Ibid, 158-60.

Chapter 14

1. Miegge, *The Virgin*, 107.
2. Graef, *Mary*, 166.
3. Ibid, 171-72.
4. Rubin, *Mother*, 174.
5. Bernard, *Bernard*, 290.
6. Ibid, 291-2.
7. Perry, *Mary*, 195.
8. Ibid, 205.
9. Ott, *Fundamentals*, 202; Graef, *Mary*, 236, 240-1.
10. *Angelus Prayer*, Card.
11. Parker, *Heaney*, 2-5.
12. Graef, *Mary*, 244, 432.
13. Ibid, 245-7.
14. Ibid, 247-8.
15. Rubin, *Mother*, 304.

Chapter 15

1. Tierney, *Crisis*, 182.
2. Graef, *Mary*, 278.
3. Ibid, 278-81.
4. Perry, *Mary*, 210-12.
5. Graef, 284.
6. Perry, *Mary*, 214-7; Graef, *Mary*, 282-6.
7. Graef, *Mary*, 287-8, Perry, *Mary*, 218-21.
8. Graef, *Mary*, 290.
9. Ibid.
10. Ibid, 290-3.
11. Graef, *Mary*, 293-5; Perry, *Mary*, 226-7.
12. Graef, *Mary*, 295-7.
13. Ibid, 299.

Chapter 16

1. Perry, *Mary*, 223.
2. Graef, *Mary*, 339.
3. Ibid.

Chapter 17

1. Graef, *Mary*, 159.
2. Rubin, *Mother*, 391.
3. Graef, *Mary*, 345-47.
4. Ibid, 347.
5. Ibid, 362.
6. Ott, *Fundamentals*, 199.
7. Miegge, *Virgin*, 21.
8. Roschini, *Maria*, 12-14.
9. Ibid, 39.
10. Ott, *Fundamentals*, 202.
11. Gambero, *Mary*, 63-4.
12. Ott, *Fundamentals*, 200-01.
13. Pelikan, *Mary*, 16.
14. Gambero, *Mary*, 114.
15. Graef, *Mary*, 181.
16. Gambero, *Mary*, 53.
17. Irenaeus, *Heresies*, 5, 19.
18. Pius XII, *Fulgens*, 7.
19. John Paul II, "Enmity," 11.
20. Ott, *Fundamentals*, 200.
21. Ibid.
22. Pelikan, *Mary*, 15.
23. Irenaeus, *Heresies*, 5.19.
24. Ott, *Fundamentals* 201.
25. Graef, *Mary*, 347-56.
26. Ibid, 356-9.
27. Ibid, 360.
28. Ibid, 378.
29. Ibid, 379.
30. Ibid, 376.
31. Ibid, 374.
32. Ibid, 386-9.
33. Perry, *Mary*, 240.
34. Pius XII, "Munificentissimus," *Thomist*, 3-21.
35. Perry, *Mary*, 243.
36. Ibid, 242.
37. Miller, *Cult*, 64.

Chapter 18

1. Allison, *Catholic Theology*, 191.
2. Guadalupe: During the two day celebration of the 478th anniversary of the apparition of the Virgin of Guadalupe, 6.1 million people were in attendance. The chapel can hold 50,000 at once. ("6.1 Pilgrims Visit Guadalupe Shrine," Zenit: The World seen from Rome [December 14, 2009]. Cited 14 March 2015. Online: http://www.zenit.org/en/articles/6-1-million-pilgrims-visit-guadalupe-shrine).
3. Lourdes: Up to five million people visit Lourdes annually. (James Hough, "How many people visit Lourdes each year?" In Catholicism [cited 14 March 2015]. Online: http://www.answers.com/Q/How_many_people_visit_Lourdes_each_year).
4. Author's Note: Personal Visit to Our Lady of San Juan Del Valle shrine, San Juan, Texas, September 14, 1968.
5. Perry, *Mary*, 247.
6. Ibid, 247.
7. Ibid, 248.
8. Laurentin, *Apparitions*, 5.
9. Miller, *Cult*, 14.
10. Ibid, 14-5.
11. Benedict XVI, *Don't Forget Mary*.
12. Francis, *Lumen*, 60.
13. Ratzinger, *Catechism*, 963-4.
14. Ibid, 2670.

Chapter 19

1. Ratzinger, *Catechism*, 85-8.
2. Ibid, 95.
3. Ibid, 111.
4. Ibid, 2051.
5. Ibid, 2037.
6. Pius XII, *Munificentissimus*, 12.
7. Ratzinger, *Catechism*, 120.
8. Ibid, 1116.
9. Ibid, 1129.
10. Ibid, 1277.
11. Ibid, 1316.
12. Ibid, 1324, 1367, 1374.
13. Ibid, 964-975.
14. Ibid, 1491-8.

15 Ibid, 1474-7.
16 Ibid, 1471-9.
17 Ibid, 964.
18 Leo XIII, *Octobri*, 196.
19 Ratzinger, *Catechism,*, 969.
20 Bernardine, *Sermo X*, a.3.c.3.
21 Author's Note: I personally attended the conference held in 2012 in Anaheim, CA. This is my own interpretation of the event.

Chapter 20

1   Geisler and MacKenzie, *Roman Catholics*, 178.
2   Manelli, *Generations*, 131-2.
3   Bock, *Luke*, 40.
4   Ratzinger, *Catechism*, 488.
5   Duff, *Blessed One*, 64.
6   Erickson, *Theology*, 640.
7   Smith, *Bible Doctrine*, 159-60.
8   Pius XII, *Munificentissimus*, 4, 5.
9   Graef, *Mary*, 43.
10 Shedd, *Theology*, "Augustine" 634-37.
11 Ibid, "Anselm," 635.
12 Ibid, "Pareus," 635.
13 Ibid, "Ursinius," 635.
14 Ibid, "Turretin," 636.
15 Shedd, *Theology*, 637.
16 Geisler, *Catholics*, 307.
17 Irenaeus, *Preaching*, 33, quoted in Pelikan, *Mary*, 190-1.
18 Ratzinger, *Catechism*, 499.
19 Ibid, 500.
20 Allison, *Catholic*, 141-42.
21 Wilkins, "Matthew," 11.
22 Vos, *Nelson's*, 450.
23 Shedd, *Theology*, 293.
24 Cyril, *Discourse*.
25 Limberis, *Heiress*, 58.

Chapter 21

1. Graef, *Mary*, 346.
2. Pius IX, *Ineffabilis Deus*.
3. Allison, *Catholic Theology*, 191.
4. Graef, *Mary*, 347.
5. Pius IX, *Ineffabilis Deus*.

Bibliography

Abraham, William J. Foreword to *Mary for Evangelicals*. By Tim Perry. Downers Grove, IL: InterVarsity Press, 2006.

Abramowski, L. *Untersuchungen zum Liber Heraclidis des Nestorius*. Subs. 22. Corpus Scriptorum Christianorum Orientalium. Belgium: Peeters Publishing, 1963.

Adams, Marilyn McCord. "The Immaculate Conception of the Blessed Virgin Mary: A Thought-Experiment in Medieval Philosophical Theology." *Harvard Theological Review* (2010): 133–59.

Allison, Gregg R. *Roman Catholic Theology and Practice: An Evangelical Assessment*. Wheaton, IL: Crossway, 2014.

Angelus Prayer. Annunciation Holy Card. Omaha, NE: Adoremus Books, 2014.

Anselm of Canterbury. *Cur Deus Homo: Why God Became Man*. Translated by Jasper Hopkins and Herbert W. Richardson. New York: E. Mellen, 1974.

Aristides, Marcianus. *The Apology of Aristides on Behalf of the Christians*. Translated by J. R. Harris. Piscataway, NJ: Gorgias Press LLC, 2004.

Augustine. "Letter 164." In *Letters 131–164*. Fathers of the Church: A New Translation Series, vol. III. Washington, DC: Catholic University of America, 1965.

Awad, Najeeb George. "'The Holy Spirit Will Come upon You': The Doctrine of the Incarnation and the Holy Spirit." *Theological Review* (2007): 23–45.

Bernard of Clairvaux. *St. Bernard of Clairvaux: Seen Through His Selected Letters*. Translated by Bruno Scott James. London: Henry Regnery, 1953.

Bernard, John Henry. "No. 19:6–10, Odes of Solomon." In *Texts and Studies: Contributions to Biblical Literature*. Cambridge, UK: Cambridge University Press, 1912.

Bock, Darrell L. *Luke*. Baker Exegetical Commentary on the New Testament. Vol. 1. Grand Rapids, MI: Baker Academic, 1994.

Borgeaud, Philippe. *Mother of the Gods: From Cybele to the Virgin Mary*. Translated by Lysa Hochroth. Baltimore, MD: Johns Hopkins University Press, 2004.

Braaten, Carl E., and Robert W. Jenson. *Mary, Mother of God*. Grand Rapids, IL: Eerdmans, 2004.

Bulgakov, Sergius. *The Burning Bush: On the Orthodox Veneration of the Mother of God*. Translated by Thomas Allen Smith. Grand Rapids, MI: Eerdmans, 2009.

Calamari, Barbara, and Sandra Dipasqua. *Visions of Mary*. New York: Harry N. Abrams, 2004.

Calvin, John. *Institutes of the Christian Religion*. Translated by Henry Beveridge. Grand Rapids, MI: Eerdmans, 1989.

Carroll, Donald. *Mary's House: The Extraordinary Story Behind the Discovery of the House Where the Virgin Mary Lived and Died*. London: Veritas Books, 2000.

Charles, R. H. *The Ascension of Isaiah: Translated from the Ethiopic Version, Which, Together With the New Greek Fragment, the Latin Versions and the Latin Translation of the Slavonic, Is Here Published in Full*. First published 1900. Reprinted, Charleston, SC: BiblioLife, 2011.

Cyril of Jerusalem. "Discourse on Mary Theotokos." In *Miscellaneous Coptic Texts in the Dialect of Upper Egypt*. Translated by E. A. W. Budge. London: British Museum, 1915.

Dadosky, John D. "Woman Without Envy: Toward Conceiving the Immaculate Conception." *Theological Studies* (2011):15–40.

Dillard, Peter S. *The Truth About Mary: A Theological and Philosophical Evaluation of the Proposed Fifth Marian Dogma*. Eugene, OR: Wipf and Stock, 2009.

Duff, Nancy. "Mary, Servant of the Lord." In *Blessed One: Protestant Perspectives on Mary*, 59–70. Edited by Beverly Roberts Gaventa and Cynthia L. Rigby. Louisville, KY: Westminster John Knox, 2002.

Dunn, Geoffrey D. "Mary's Virginity In Partu and Tertullian's Anti-Docetism in De Carne Christi Reconsidered." *Journal of Theological Studies* (2007):467–84.

Elder, E. Rozanne. "Macula Nigra et Virgo Immaculata: Bernard's Tests for True Doctrine." *Cistercian Studies Quarterly* (2003):423–38.

Elliott, J. K. "The Protevangelium of James." In *The Apocryphal New Testament*, 48–67. Translated by M. R. James. Oxford: Clarendon Press, 1993.

Erickson, Millard J. *Christian Theology*. 2nd ed. Grand Rapids, MI: Baker, 1998.

Eusebius. *Life of Constantine*. Translated by Averil Cameron and Stewart G. Hall. Clarendon Ancient History Series. New York: Oxford University Press, 1999.

Frank, Franz Hermann Reinhold. *System of Christian Certainty*. Edinburgh: T & T Clark, 1886.

Fuller, Reginald C., Leonard Johnston, and Conleth Kearns, ed. *A New Catholic Commentary on Holy Scripture*. Camden, NJ: Thomas Nelson, Inc., 1969.

Gambero, Luigi. *Mary and the Fathers of the Church: The Blessed Virgin in Patristic Thought*. San Francisco: Ignatius Press, 1999.

Geisler, Norman L., and Ralph E. Mackenzie. *Roman Catholics and Evangelicals: Agreements and Differences*. Grand Rapids, MI: Baker, 1995.

Graef, Hilda, and Thomas A. Thompson. *Mary: A History of Doctrine and Devotion*. Notre Dame, IN: Ave Maria Press, 2009.

Hahn, Scott. *Hail Holy Queen: The Mother of God in the Word of God*. New York: Doubleday, 2001.

Heine, Ronald E. *Origen: Commentary on the Book of John*. Fathers of the Church: A New Translation, books 13–32. Washington, DC: Catholic University Press, 1993.

Henry, Matthew. *Genesis to Deuteronomy*. Matthew Henry's Commentary on the Whole Bible, vol. 1. Peabody, Mass.: Hendrickson, 1996.

Holum, Kenneth G. *Theodosian Empresses: Women and Imperial Dominion in Late Antiquity*. Transformation of the Classical Heritage, book 3. Berkeley, CA: University of California Press, 1989.

Hough, James. "How many people visit Lourdes each year?" *Catholicism*. Accessed March 14, 2015. http://www.answers.com/Q/How_many_people_visit_Lourdes_each_year.

Hislop, Alexander. *The Two Babylons: The Papal Worship Proved to Be the Worship of Nimrod and His Wife*. 1903. Reprint, Lexington, KY: Forgotten Books, 2012.

Ignatius. "Epistle to the Ephesians." In *Ante-Nicene Fathers: The Writings of the Fathers Down to A.D. 325, Volume I—The Apostolic Fathers with Justin Martyr and Irenaeus*, pp. 45–49. Edited by Alexander Roberts, James Donaldson, and Arthur Cleveland Coxe. New York: Cosmo, 2007.

———. "Epistle to the Trallians." *Ante-Nicene Fathers: The Writings of the Fathers Down to A.D. 325, Volume I - The Apostolic Fathers with Justin Martyr and Irenaeus*, pp. 66–72. Edited by Alexander Roberts, James Donaldson, and Arthur Cleveland Coxe. New York: Cosmo, 2007.

Irenaeus. *Against Heresies*. Anti-Nicene Fathers, vol. 1. Edited by A. Cleveland Coxe. Peabody, MA: Hendrickson, 1999.

———. *Proof of Apostolic Preaching*. Translated by Joseph P. Smith. Ancient Christian Writers, book 16. Mahwah, NJ: Paulist, 1978.

John Paul II. "Mary's Enmity Toward Satan Was Absolute." *L'Osservatore Romano*, June 5, 1996.

"John Chrysostom." *Oxford Dictionary of Byzantium*, vol. 1. Edited by Alexander Kazhdan. New York: Oxford University Press, 1991.

Justin Martyr. *Dialogue With Trypho*. Translated by Thomas B. Falls. Selections of the Fathers of the Church, vol. 3. Edited by Michael Slusser. Washington, DC: Catholic University Press, 2003.

Karweise, Stefan. "The Church of Mary and the Temple of Hadrian Olympios." In *Ephesos: Metropolis of Asia*. Edited by Helmut Koester. Cambridge, MA: Harvard University Press, 1995.

Labooy, Guus. "The Historicity of the Virginal Conception. A Study in Argumentation." *European Journal of Theology* (2004): 91–101.

Lane, Anthony. *A Concise History of Christian Thought*. Grand Rapids, MI: Baker Academic, 2006.

Laurentin, Rene. *The Apparitions of the Blessed Virgin Mary Today*. Translated by Luke Griffin. Dublin: Veritas, 1990.

Leo XIII. *Octobri Mense Adventante*. Encyclical, *Ass24*. September 22, 1891.

Limberis, Vasiliki. *Divine Heiress: The Virgin Mary and the Creation of Christian Constantinople*. New York: Routledge, 1994.

Longenecker, Dwight, and David Gustafson. *Mary: A Catholic – Evangelical Debate*. Grand Rapids, MI: Brazos Press, 2003.

Loofs, Friedrich. *Nestoriana: die Fragmente des Nestorius*. Halle, Germany: Max Niemeyer, 1904.

Loofs, Friedrich. *Nestorius and His Place in the History of Christian Doctrine*. Cambridge, UK: Cambridge University Press, 1914.

MacQuarrie, John. *Mary for All Christians*. New York: T & T Clark Ltd., 2001.

Malalas, John. *Chronographia*. Translated by Elizabeth Jeffreys, Michael Jeffreys, and Roger Scott. Melbourne: Australian Association for Byzantine Studies, 1986.

Manelli, Stefano M. *All Generations Shall Call Me Blessed: Biblical Mariology*. Translated by Peter Damien Fehlner. New Bedford, MA: Academy of the Immaculate, 1995.

Marshall, I. Howard, and W. Ward Gasque, ed. *The Gospel of Luke*. New International Greek New Testament Commentary. Grand Rapids, MI: Eerdmans, 1978.

Miegge, Giovanni. *The Virgin Mary*. Translated by Waldo Smith. Philadelphia, PA: Westminster Press, 1955.

Mikhail, Labib. *The Virgin Mary in the Light of the Word of God*. Translated by Nasser S. Farag. Ventura, CA: Nordskog Publishing, 2011.

Miller, Elliot, and Kenneth R. Samples. *The Cult of the Virgin: Catholic Mariology and the Apparitions of Mary*. Grand Rapids, MI: Baker, 1992.

Mulder Jr., Jack. "Why More Christians Should Believe in Mary's Immaculate Conception." *Christian Scholar's Review* (2012): 117–34.

Mussolini, Mauro. "The Rise of the New Civic Ritual of the Immaculate Conception of the Virgin in Sixteenth-Century Siena." *Renaissance Studies* (2006): 253–75.

Nawatu, Felix. "The Immaculate Conception: A Model of the Development of Dogma." *Asia Journal of Theology* (2009): 3–21.

Ott, Ludwig. *Fundamentals of Catholic Dogma*. Edited by James Canon Bastible. Translated by Patrick Lynch. Saint Louis, MO: Herder, 1954.

Painter, John. "ARCIC on Mary: An Historical Consideration of the Use of Early Church Evidence in the Seattle Statement." *Journal of Anglican Studies* (2006): 59–80.

Parker, Michael. *Seamus Heaney: The Making of the Poet*. Basingstoke, England: MacMillan, 1993.

Pelikan, Jaroslav. *Mary Through the Centuries: Her Place in the History of Culture*. New Haven, CT: Yale, 1996.

Perry, Tim. *Mary for Evangelicals: Toward an Understanding of the Mother of Our Lord*. Downers Grove, IL: InterVarsity Press, 2006.

Palladius. *Dialogus de Vita Joannis Chrysostomi*. Edited by P. R. Coleman-Norton. *Palladi Dialugus de vita S. Joanni Chrysostomi*. Cambridge, UK: Cambridge University Press, 1928.

Pius IX. *Ineffabilis Deus*. Translated by Claudia Carlen Ihm. The Papal Encyclicals 1740 to 1981, vol. 1. Ypsilanti, MI: Pierian, 1990.

Pius XII. *Fulgens Corona*. Vatican City: Libreria Editrice Vaticana, 1953.

———. "Munificentissimus Deus." Translated by Joseph C. Fenton. *The Thomist* 14 (1951): 3–21.

Ratzinger, John Cardinal. *Catechism of the Catholic Church*. 2nd ed. Vatican City: Libreria Editrice Vaticana, 1997.

Riches, Aaron. "Deconstructing the Linearity of Grace: The Risk and Reflexive Paradox of Mary's Immaculate Fiat." *International Journal of Systematic Theology* (2008): 179–94.

Roschini, Gabriele M. *Chi e Maria? Catechismo Mariano*. Rome: Edizioni Paoline, 1954.

Rubin, Miri. *Mother of God: History of the Virgin Mary*. New Haven, CT: Yale, 2009.

Schnittjer, Gary Edward. *The Torah Story: An Apprenticeship on the Pentateuch*. Grand Rapids, MI: Zondervan, 2006.

Shedd, William G. T. *Dogmatic Theology*. 3rd ed. Edited by Alan W. Gomes. Phillipsburg, NJ: Presbyterian and Reformed Publishing, 2003.

Sisto, Walter N. "Marian Dogmas and Reunion: What Eastern Catholics Can Teach Us About Catholic Ecumenism." *Journal of Ecumenical Studies* (2011): 150–62.

Smith, Charles Ryder. *The Bible Doctrine of Sin and the Ways of God with Sinners*. London: Epworth, 1953.

Socrates Scholasticus. *Ecclesiastical History.* Translated by A. C. Zenos. Nicene and Post-Nicene Fathers. 2nd series, vol. 2. Edited by Philip Schaff and Henry Wace. Buffalo, NY: Christian Literature Publishing Co., 1890. Revised and edited for New Advent by Kevin Knight. http://www.newadvent.org/fathers/2601.htm.

Sozomen. *Ecclesiastical History.* Nicene and Post-Nicene Fathers. 2nd series, vol. 2. Edited by Philip Schaff and Henry Wace. Peabody, MA: Hendrickson, 1996.

———. *History of the Church in Nine Books.* Translated by Samuel Bagster and Sons. London: Aterna Press, 2014.

Stein, Robert H. *Luke.* The New American Commentary, vol. 24. Nashville, TN: Broadman Press, 1992.

Tierney, Brian. *The Crisis of Church and State, 1050–1300.* Medieval Academy Reprints for Teaching. Reprint, Englewood, CO: Prentice-Hall, 1964.

Vos, Howard F. *Nelson's New Illustrated Bible Manners and Customs.* Nashville, TN: Thomas Nelson, 1999.

Waltke, Bruce K., and Cathi Fredricks. *Genesis: A Commentary.* Grand Rapids, MI: Zondervan, 2001.

Wilkins, Michael J. "Matthew." In *Zondervan Illustrated Bible Backgrounds Commentary*, vol. 1. Edited by Clinton E. Arnold. Grand Rapids, MI: Zondervan, 2002.

Wenham, Gordon J. *Word Biblical Commentary, Genesis 1–15.* Camden, NJ: Thomas Nelson, Inc., 1987.

Zenit: The World Seen from Rome. "6.1 Pilgrims Visit Guadalupe Shrine." Accessed Mary 14, 2015. http://www.zenit.org/en/articles/6-1-million-pilgrims-visit-guadalupe-shrine.

APPENDIX

CHAIRETISMOI HYMN

Hail full of grace, unreaped soil of heavenly grain.
Hail full of grace, undeceitful Virgin Mother of the true vine.
Hail full of grace, unfailing net of the immutable Godhead.
Hail full of grace, wide open field of the undivided nature.
Hail full of grace, oh unsustained bearer, bride of the bereaved world.
Hail full of grace, the weaver of the crown, which was not braided by hand, and was made for creation.
Hail full of grace, the house of holy fire.
Hail full of grace, you are the return for those who fled the world.
Hail full of grace, you are the undepletable treasury of the world.
Hail full of grace. The joy from you, Holy Virgin, is infinite.
Hail full of grace, you are adorned with many virtues, you are the torch-bearing light, and the inextinguishable light brighter than the sun.